The Merrill Studies
in
The Octopus

CHARLES E. MERRILL STUDIES

Under the General Editorship of
Matthew J. Bruccoli and Joseph Katz

The Merrill Studies
in
The Octopus

Compiled by
Richard Allan Davison
University of Delaware

Charles E. Merrill Publishing Company
A Bell & Howell Company
Columbus, Ohio

Standard Book Number: 675-09408-9

Library of Congress Catalog Number: 79-93996

1 2 3 4 5 6 7 8 9 10 — 78 77 76 75 74 73 72 71 70 69

Printed in the United States of America

Preface

On December 15, 1900, shortly after he had completed *The Octopus*, Frank Norris described his most ambitious literary project: "The Trilogy of The Epic of the Wheat will include the following novels: *The Octopus*, a Story of California; *The Pit*, a Story of Chicago; *The Wolf*, a Story of Europe . . . involving (1) the production, (2) the distribution, (3) the consumption of American wheat. When complete they will form the story of a crop of wheat from the time of its sowing as seed in California to the time of its consumption as bread in a village of Western Europe." By October 25, 1902, Norris was dead, with only the first two novels of the projected trilogy written.

This collection of statements on *The Octopus*, Norris' most impressive novel, is in part a tribute to a genius so untimely curtailed. It is also a living record of the excitement, the controversy, the critical ingenuity that such a gigantic work has engendered. In surveying almost seventy years of criticism on *The Octopus* I have encountered (along with intellectual scrupulousness and some dishonesty) much disagreement as to both artistic detail and philosophical scope. While one critic calls the novel masterfully structured yet philosophically inconsistent, another sees philosophical consistency but flawed structure. To a single critic's eyes the novel is both a literary chaos and a fine overall achievement. There has been praise and condemnation by critics whose readings encompass aspects from poetic justice to social Darwinism. Critics have seen melodrama and tragedy. Perhaps the only constant in all the commentary is in the enthusiastic acknowledgment of the power and scope of *The Octopus*. Norris' novel has been widely read for many decades and is presently available in numerous editions. Today it remains, more than ever, a novel to be reckoned with. I have tried to collect the best available criticism on *The Octopus* that is varied, intelligent, and that will, at best, prompt a rereading of Norris' novel. The materials are arranged in chronological sequence, so that the reader can see how most of the critics have affected each other as well as how they all have been affected by *The Octopus*.

My thanks to Miss Kathleen A. McKinley for her aid as my research assistant. My special thanks to Professor Harry Hayden Clark for stimulating my interest in the writings of Frank Norris.

RAD

Contents

1. Letters by Frank Norris

2. Reviews of *The Octopus*

3. Criticism and Scholarship

1. Letters by Frank Norris

To Harry M. Wright

April 5, 1899: Wednesday

My Dear Harry:

. . . I am leaving for California Monday next to be gone, very likely
until fall. It has happened quite unexpectedly, but is the result
of a talk I had with the firm here. They believe with me that the
big American novel is going to come out of the West — California.
They have an idea that I can write it and it would be cruel and
heartless to disillusion em. I've got an idea thats as big as all
out-doors & McClure is going to back me up while I put it through
and me pay goes marching on the whiles. It involves a very long,
very serious and perhaps a very terrible novel. It will be all about
the San Joaquin wheat raisers and the Southern Pacific, and I
guess we'll call it The Octopus. — catch on? I mean to study the
whole question as faithfully as I can and then write a hair lifting
story. Theres the chance for the big, Epic, dramatic thing in this,
and I mean to do it thoroughly.—get at it from every point of view,
the social, agricultural, & political. Just say the last word on the
R. R. question in California. I am going to study the whole thing
on the ground, and come back here in the winter and make a novel
out of it. What do you think of the idea. . . .

Reprinted from the Letters of Frank Norris, Franklin Walker, ed., (San
Francisco: The Book Club of California, 1956), 35, 47-48, 67-68.

To Isaac F. Marcosson

My dear Marcosson:

Yours of the 18th to hand and am glad to get it. If you have been involved in politics recently, perhaps you can give me a pointer or two. I am in a beautiful 'political muddle' myself in 'The Octopus,' the first of my set of three novels on the wheat question, which I have just started. You know this involves, in California, the fight between the farmers of the San Joaquin and the Southern Pacific Railroad. I was out there this summer getting what stuff I needed but I did not think I should need political notes. Now, I find that I do, and should have got 'em long ago. I have gone to work on this and have found out a good deal about politics and political 'deals' but I want to find out more.

The situation in my story is this: There is a certain group of farmers who, despairing of ever getting fair freight rates from the Railroad or of electing a board of Railroad Commissioners by fair means themselves, set about gaining their ends by any means available. What they want to do is to cause the nomination and election of railroad commissioners of their own choosing, with the idea that these commissioners will make proper reductions in freight rates. They are prepared to spend a very large amount of money to accomplish this. They want to put the deal through just among themselves, because they have tried to organise the rest of

the farmers in the State and have failed. I think they form a kind
of a ring of six or eight men. They are all fairly rich men, but are
in a pretty desperate situation, the railroad having pushed them
to just about the limit.

Can you tell me just about how they would go about to get
their men in? Do you think it could be done at all? What I am
anxious to get hold of are the *details* of this kind of game, the
lingo, and the technique, etc., but at the same time, want to understand it very clearly.

Can you give me any idea of how this sort of deal would be put
through. If you can help me along I should be no end obliged.

The next book of mine to appear is the 'Man's Woman.' It is
scheduled for about the last week in February. It's a kind of
theatrical sort with a lot of niggling analysis to try to justify the
violent action of the first few chapters. It is very slovenly put
together and there are only two real people in all its 100,000 words.
It's different from my other books, but it's the last one that will
be, if you understand what I mean. I am going back definitely
now to the style of MacT. and stay with it right along. I've been
sort of feeling my way ever since the 'Moran' days and getting a
twist of myself. Now I think I know where I am at and what game
I play the best. The Wheat series will be straight naturalism with
all the guts I can get into it.

Yours very sincerely,
Frank Norris

To Isaac F. Marcosson

Sept. 13, 1900

My dear I.F.M.

Your breathless note — written while you ran, I verily believe —is before me. I caught it on the fly.

The Squid is nearing conclusion. Hooray! I can see the end. It is the hardest work I ever have done in my life, a solid year of writing and 4 months preparation—bar two months— and I think the best thing far and away I ever did. You've no idea of the outside work on it. I've been in correspondence with all kinds of people during its composition, from the Traffic Manager of a Western railroad to the sub-deputy-assistant of the Secretary of Agriculture at Washington. Also in connection with it all I've helped run and work a harvester in the San Joaquin—that is I helped on the sacking-platform—but of course you don't know where that is. Well, the thing is mostly done now and I known when it slumps and I know when it strikes and I think the strikes are the most numerous and important. I know that in the masses I've made no mistake. You will find some things in it that for me—are new departures. It is the most romantic thing I've yet done. One of the secondary sub-plots is pure romance—oh, even mysticism, if you like, a sort of allegory— I call it the allegorical side of the wheat subject—and the fire in it is the Allegory of the Wheat. The movement of the whole business is very slow at first—don't really get under weigh till after the first 15,000 words (it's about 200,000 words long), then, with the first pivotal incident it quickens a bit, and from there on I've tried to accelerate it steadily till at the last you are—I hope—just whirling and galloping and tearing along till you come *bang!* all of a sudden to a great big crushing END, something that will slam you right between your eyes and knock you off your feet—all this I *hope* for. Sabe? There will be about 20 characters in the book, 10 really important, 10 (about) secondary and five or six more supers. In the front matter I am going —maybe—to insert a list of dramatis personae and—This *surely* —a map of the locality.

Such a long letter. You did not deserve it.

Frank Norris

2.   Reviews of *The Octopus*

Wallace Rice

Norris "The Octopus"

Frank Norris has written a novel, as fascinating, as repellent, as multifarious, as misshapen as the marine monster from which it gains its name of "The Octopus" (Doubleday, Page & Co.). Sufficiently absorbing to hold the reader with something of the Wedding Guest's insistence, once it is taken up, it leaves him with precisely the opposite impression with which Coleridge's masterpiece is laid down. It is wonderfully clever, and only where the author permits himself vain repetitions does its interest flag; but its philosophy is hideous, and the book is as certainly at war with itself as its characters are with one another. To its composition every crime lends its bad interest—rape, murder, train robbing, bribery, corruption in politics, prostitution, inordinate greed, lust for gold and lust for blood. In his characters, for the most part, vice is rebuked and morality upheld. To those who depart from the accepted standard, romantic justice, as unusual in life as it becomes customary here, is meted out with fine particularity. The bad man is killed with a rifle shot, the train robber is sentenced for life, the

Reprinted from *Chicago American Literary and Art Review* (April 6, 1901), 5-6.

briber goes down into the darkness of insanity, the corruption-monger is strangled in his own accumulating wealth. Everywhere Mr. Norris shows himself to be animated by high principle in his treatment of his characters. But in the underlying principles which he demonstrates at the end, the babyish plea of elemental force and destiny is entered for the arch-devil of them all, and the other lessons go for naught.

"The Octopus," like Mr. Norris' other well-known books, is a work of realism. Its foundation facts are derived from the history of the Southern Pacific Railroad, and almost all the story revolves around the machinations of the officials of that great monopoly. In this the author becomes a public benefactor—at least in intention. How difficult it will be for him to persuade Americans of the substantial truth of his indictment against such a corporation may be known to him, yet the fate which befell Messrs. Merwin and Webster's "The Short-Line War" two years ago will be interesting in this connection. The two authors came upon an attempt on the part of Jay Gould to grab one of the feeders of the Erie Railway, an independent company, as it appeared in the records of one of the courts in New York State. Finding the account more fascinating than anything they could plan for themselves, they made a careful investigation, and in writing the romance held themselves closely to the demonstrable facts.

The book was read by one of the leading officials of the Burlington Road at my instance, and he told me afterward that he himself had been through precisely such an experience in the West, identical with the narrative to such an extent that he knew every move of the warring factions in the corporation before he reached them. In the face of this, in spite of the double occurrence of just such depredations as the book disclosed, the New York Evening Post dismissed the story as incredible—the New York Evening Post at that time being controlled by the Villard interests. Mr. Norris makes a far more serious indictment against the Southern Pacific than this. He quotes actual documents to prove the wickedness of the position taken by its officials in ousting the men whom it induced to settle on its lands by what turned out to be the falsest of false pretenses; but he does not stop there. The Octopus has as many branches as its namesake. It controls the Railway Commission, it controls the Legislature, it controls the courts. In drawing his indictment against it in the earlier part of the book Mr. Norris does unconsciously the thing he represents the commissioners as doing corruptly; he raises his rate so high that it is certain to be

rejected at the bar of public opinion. If his novel be one with a
purpose, and that the exposure of infinitely corrupt corporation
methods, it is self-defeated on the instant. He himself seems aware
of this later in the book, for his most intimate character says: "Tell
the people five years from now the story of the fight between the
League of San Joaquin and the railroad and it will not be believed."

This is the chief fault to be found with the construction of
the book—and a book with a self-defeated purpose can hardly be
called a book at all, even though, as here, it abounds in vivid
descriptions, insistent characterizations and abounding interest.
There are other faults, more noticeable in a book serving so realistic
a purpose than in any other. Priests of the Roman Church do not
quote the Protestant translations of the Scriptures, for example,
as Father Serria does here. The episode of Vanamee and Angele
Varian, poetic and engrossing though it be, has no possible relevance in this work, nor is it in any way bound up in the rest of it.
The sandwiching of the account of the dinner in the house of a
millionaire and of the starving of a mother in the street is felt to
be a trick, a tour de force, rather than literature—the literature
that Mr. Norris affects to despise in more than one place in his
pages, as though his book could have illiterary vitality.

But, as was intimated before, the philosophy of the book is its
weakest point. After all the sin and suffering and death of its earlier
pages, the whole question of personal responsibility for crime is
dismissed by the archfiend of them all in these words: "Try to
believe this—to begin with—that railroads build themselves. Where
there is demand, sooner or later there will be a supply. Mr. Derrick,
does he grow his wheat? The wheat grows itself. What does he
count for? Does he supply the force? What do I count for? Do I
build the railroad? You are dealing with forces, young man, when
you speak of wheat and the railroad, not with men. There is the
wheat, the supply. It must be carried to feed the people. There
is the demand. The wheat is one force, the railroad another, and
there is the law that governs them—supply and demand. Men have
only little to do in the whole business. Complications may arise,
conditions that bear hard on the individual—crush him maybe—
but the wheat will be carried to feed the people as inevitably as
it will grow. Blame conditions, not men."

It need not be pointed out that this hideous doctrine, the doctrine that would justify a Nero and damn an Antonine, can be
urged in favor of any crime that ever was hatched in warped and
brutal brains. It is the doctrine of personal irresponsibility, of a

conscienceless world, of a godless universe. It is the plea of organized greed and unrestrained lust in all ages. Most unfortunately
it is the plea which Mr. Norris represents as wholly converting the
most intelligent character in his book, the character with which he
asserts the greatest degree of personal intimacy and for which he
makes the greatest appeal for the reader's sympathy.

Frederic T. Cooper

Frank Norris' *The Octopus*

There is a character at the outset of Mr. Norris's new volume, the poet Presley, who is haunted by the dream of writing an epic of the West. His ambition is to paint life frankly as he sees it; yet, incongruously enough, he wishes to see everything through a rose-tinted mist—a mist that will tone down all the harsh outlines and crude colours. He is searching for true romance, and, instead, finds himself continually brought up against railway tracks and grain rates and unjust freight tariffs. All this is quite interesting, not because Presley is an especially important or convincing character, but because it is so obviously only another way of stating Mr. Norris's favourite creed: that realism and romanticism are, after all, convertible terms; that the epic theme for which Presley was vainly groping lay all the time close at hand if he could but have seen it, not merely in the primeval life of mountain and desert, and the shimmering purple of a sunset, but in the limitless stretch of steel rails, in the thunder of passing trains, in the whole vast, intricate mechanism of an organised monopoly.

No one is likely to quarrel seriously with this position. There certainly is a sort of epic vastness and power in many phases of

Reprinted from *Bookman*, XIII (May 1901), 245-47.

our complicated modern life when treated in a broad, sweeping Zolaesque fashion—in the railroad, the stock exchange, the department stores when they are set before us like so many vast symbols, titanic organisms, with an entity and a purpose of their own. It is only when we come down to details, the petty, sordid details of individual lives, that realism and romance part company. Yet no one knows better than Mr. Norris that it is these very details which give to every picture of life its true value and colour, and he himself has often given them to us with pitiless fidelity. There are few writers of to-day who could cope with him in giving the physiognomy of some mean little side-street in San Francisco, of painting with a few telling strokes a living picture of some odd little Chinese restaurant, of making us breathe the very atmosphere of McTeague's tawdry, disordered, creosote-laden dental parlour, or the foul, reeking interior of Bennett's tent on the ice fields of the far North. It is a trifle exasperating to find a man who can do work like this deliberately choosing every now and then, after the fashion of his poet Presley, to look at life through rose-coloured glasses, instead of adhering fearlessly to the crude colours and the harsh outlines. It was this tendency which betrayed him into the melodramatic ending of *McTeague;* in real life the big, dull-witted dentist would probably have perished miserably in a gutter or a garret, if he had succeeded in evading the hangman; but it suited Mr. Norris's purpose better to apotheosise him, to drive him out into the midst of the alkali desert, forming, as it were, the one human note in a sort of vast symphony of nature. In the present work there is nothing quite so glaring, yet we detect the same underlying spirit. It is felt not alone in the vein of mysticism which runs through the book, the whole episode of Vanamee, the lonely, half-distraught shepherd invoking the spirit of his lost bride across the wide expanse of prairie. It is felt still more in the lack of vivid character drawing in *The Octopus,* in a certain blurring of the outlines, that suggests a composite photograph, in the substitution of types for individuals. In more than one way Mr. Norris is farther away from real life in *The Octopus* than he was in *A Man's Woman,* just as in that novel he was farther away than in *McTeague.*

The truth is that *The Octopus* is a sort of vast allegory, an example of symbolism pushed to the extreme limit, rather than a picture of life. Mr. Norris has always had a fondness for big themes; they are better suited to the special qualities of his style, the sonority of his sentences, the insistent force of accumulated

noun and adjective. This time he has conceived the ambitious idea
of writing a trilogy of novels which, taken together, shall symbolise
American life, not merely the life of some small corner of a single
State, but American life as a whole, with all its hopes and aspira-
tions and its tendencies, throughout the length and breadth of
the continent. And for the central symbol he has taken wheat, as
being quite literally and truly the staff of this life, the ultimate
source of American power and prosperity. This first volume, *The
Octopus*, dealing with the production of wheat, shows us a corner
of California, the San Joachin Valley, where a handful of ranch-
men are engaged in irrigating and ploughing, planting, reaping and
harvesting, performing all the slow, arduous toil of cultivation, and
at the same time carrying on a continuous warfare against the
persistent encroachment of the railroad, whose steel arms are
reaching out, octopus-like, the grasp, encircle and crush one after
another all those who venture to oppose it. It is quite likely that
Mr. Norris has been careful of his facts, that he has some basis
for his presentment of the railway's acts of aggression, the unjust
increase of freight tariffs, the regrading of land values, the violent
evictions—in short, that his novel is well documented. From the
symbolic side, however, the literal truth is unimportant. The novel
typifies on a small scale the struggle continuously going on between
capital and labour, the growth of centralised power, the aggression
of the corporation and the trust. But back of the individual, back
of the corporation, is the spirit of the nation, typified in the wheat,
unchanged, indomitable, rising, spreading, gathering force, rolling
in a great golden wave from West to East, across the continent,
across the ocean, and carrying with it health and strength and hope
and sustenance to other nations—emblem of the progressive, indomitable spirit of the American people. Such, at least, seems to
be Mr. Norris's underlying thought, and he has developed it in a
way which compels admiration, even from those who find *The
Octopus* as a story rather disappointing. Especially deserving of
cordial praise is the manner in which the two underlying thoughts
of his theme are kept before the reader, like the constantly recur-
ring *leitmotivs* of a Wagnerian opera. First, there is the *motiv* of
the railroad, insistent, aggressive, refusing to be forgotten, making
its presence felt on every page of the book—in the shrill scream of
a distant engine, in the heavy rumble of a passing freight train, in
the substantial presence of S. Behrmann, the local agent, whose
name greets us at the outset of the story in large flaring letters
of a painted sign on a water-tank, "S. Behrmann has something

to say to *you*," and whose corpulent, imperturbable, grasping personality obtrudes itself continually, placid, unyielding, invincible. Now and then we have a clear-cut picture of the road itself, as in the graphic, ghastly episode of an engine, ploughing its way through a flock of sheep, which had somehow made their way through the barbed-wire fence and wandered upon the track. . . .

Such, in brief, are the purposes of Mr. Norris's book. It is full of enthusiasm and poetry and conscious strength. One can hardly read it without a responsive thrill of sympathy for the earnestness, the breadth of purpose, the verbal power of the man. But as a study of character, a picture of real life, of flesh and blood, it must be frankly owned that *The Octopus* is disappointing. A few of the characters are good, they promise at first to win our sympathies— characters like the slow, tenacious German, Hooven; the tall, commanding figure of Magnus Derrick, the "governor," to whom life was one huge gamble; the coarse-fibred, combative young farmer, Annixter, with his scorn of "feemales" and his morbid concern over the vagaries of a stomach which would persist in "getting out of whack." But, taken as a whole, the characters do not wear well; they come and go, love and suffer and die, and their joy and their misery fail to wake a responsive thrill. An exception, however, must be made in the case of S. Behrmann. He, at least, is consistently developed and consistently hated. From first to last he has appeared invincible, out of reach of law, of powder and shot, of dynamite. And the final episode, where he is struck down at the very summit of his ambition, caught in a trap by his own wheat, and pictured writhing, struggling, choking to death miserably in the dark hold of the ship, beaten down and lashed by the pitiless hail of grain as it pours with a metallic roar from the iron chute, is a chapter tense with dramatic power—a scene for which a parallel must be sought in the closing pages of *Germinal* or the episode of the man-hunt in *Paris*. Whatever shortcomings *The Octopus* may possess, this one chapter goes far toward atoning for them. It gives a glimpse of Mr. Norris at his best, and holds out a hopeful promise for the future volumes of the trilogy.

Anonymous

An Epic of Wheat

... Two sub-plots hold our interest: the delicate love Idyll of
Vanamee and Angéle Varian, touching upon phases of the most
modern phsychological thought, the shadowy world of the mind, and
the wholesome romance, fresh, simple, strong, natural, between
"Buck" Annister and Hilma Tree. He is an aggressively masculine,
youthful, obstinate, healthy animal, reclaimed through his love
for her beauty, purity, and good sense. In Hilma, Mr. Norris shows
again how well he can portray a beautiful woman. In this he is
easily the peer of Kipling. In fact, we doubt if that great writer of
short stories will ever write a novel which in the handling of complex forces in modern life, creation of character, or realism, will
equal "The Octopus."

Shelgrim, the President of the Road, playing the part of spider
in his den in the midst of the system he has created, though
remarkable appears only in a very small portion of the story: which
is for the most part placed in a region of ranches, of which the
largest is called Los Muestos, down in the San Joaquin Valley, not
more than a day away from San Francisco. The life on the ranches

---

Reprinted from *Overland Monthly, XXXVII* (May 1901), 1050-1051.

16

until consumed by the Octopus, is of an easy-going, out-door, good-natured sort. Annister lies in a hammock on his porch eating prunes and reading David Copperfield; he marries the daughter of his dairy keeper; the big dance he gives in his great barn is a tremendous rollicking affair, interrupted by the entrance of a farm-hand on horseback, who fights a duel, there and then, with the proprietor, and which is enlivened by a punch so strong as to be popularly dubbed "the fertilizer." "But Presley," Mrs. Derrick murmured when he explained to her his "Song of the West," whose truth, savagery, nobility, heroism, and obscenity had revolted her, "that is not literature." "No," he had cried between his teeth, "no, thank God, it is not." But it is life, we add. There is life in the personality of Hilma Tree, from which "there was disengaged a vibrant note of gaiety, of exuberant animal life, sane, honest, strong." There is life in the unscrupulous, ambitious, fashionably garbed figure of Lyman Derrick, the young San Francisco lawyer. . . . The situations as depicted in Mr. Norris' virile, trenchant, galvanized phrase, is well worth serious attention. Whether or not one agrees with Presley's conclusion that "men were naught, death was naught, life was naught; Force only existed—Force that brought men into the world, Force that crowded them out of it to make way for the succeeding generation, Force that made the wheat grow, Force that garnered it from the soil to give place to the succeeding crop."

Anonymous

The Octopus

. . . If the author has any political doctrines, they are not clearly defined. He simply dramatizes a tragic situation. Apparently he has been shocked into an impression of Western life with its monstrous quickenings and vast travails; and he writes under the impetus of a strong and morbid excitement. The flaw in the book is that too much emphasis at the beginning has destroyed the possibility of proper emphasis at the close. The author has not enough personal self-restraint for his theme. He grows a trifle hysterical in the end. Sorrow is overdone. Justice fails him, and he unconsciously appeals to the mob for sympathy.

But *The Octopus* has qualities that lift it out of the rank of commonplace fiction. There is a breadth in the conception like the bigness that pervades the West. It takes in comedy and tragedy, nature and man, the tender heart and the inexorable law, the little home and the world, the grain of wheat and the big, warm earth that enfolds it, the railroad and the sheep crushed upon its track. The earth is as much a character in the story as any other. The author has earthy instincts and powers of interpretation that give life and meanings profound to the clods beneath his feet. He clears away everything but the earth and sky and his *dramatis persona*. The effect is tremendous, but it is not the power of true art. The final impression on the reader is that the individual

Reprinted from *Independent,* LIII (May 16, 1901), 1139-1140.

human will has no sway or freedom, but is beaten down by inanimate force. Mr. Norris expresses the idea in his own vigorous language thus:

> "Colossal indifference only, a vast trend toward appointed goals. Nature was, there, a gigantic enigma, a vast cyclopean power, huge, terrible, a leviathan with a heart of steel, knowing no compunction, no forgiveness, no tolerance; crushing out the human atoms standing in its way, with Nirvanic calm, the agony of destruction sending never a jar, never the faintest tremor, through all the prodigious mechanism of wheels and cogs."

No better comment on the last impression of the book could be written. It is our favorite contention that the aim of art is to enlarge the human will, not to contract it. In this enlargement lie both the joy and the morality of true literature.

As for the men in this world of "wheels and cogs," their hearts are with the wheat in the earth. They affect neither virtue nor modesty, and their humor is Brobdingnagian. They are coarse and vital, and, but for the author's obsession by the demon of blind force, might have stood forth as elemental human beings. As it is, the author's own lack of balance enters too deeply into their composition. Annixter is at the first a unique and powerful creation; but his sudden conversion to domestic modesty is grotesquely contrary to human nature; it is the handiwork of a man inexperienced in life. To offset the brutal materialism of his world Mr. Norris has introduced into his society two romantic characters—a poet and a seer. The poet is intended to sustain the same relations to the story as were held by the chorus in the old Greek tragedies. He interprets for the reader by struggling to understand conditions himself. The conception is a good one, but made somewhat ineffective by the crude contrasts in the situation and by a failure to comprehend the true poetic nature. The idea of his great poem which stirs the nation is evidently borrowed from the widely bruited doggerel verse called "The Man with the Hoe." The mysterious seer is well and powerfully drawn in the earlier chapters, but dwindles away somehow into regions of the most artificial and unconvincing supernaturalism. . . .

. . . despite its manifold crudities, this book contains scenes of real beauty, and elements of power that only need to put off hysterical license to rival anything written in recent years. What the author needs most is not ideas, but the temper and patience of a calmer and more massive personality.

William M. Payne

A Review of *The Octopus*

Mr. Frank Norris has evidently determined to become the American Zola. The brutal realism of his first books indicated a marked intention of following in the footsteps of his French prototype, and all that was needed to make the parallel complete was the invention of some large scheme of social portrayal which should link together a series of semi-independent novels. Such a scheme he has now elaborated. . . .

. . . Mr. Norris has dealt with its first phase in a manner that cannot fail to win respect and even admiration, in spite of the defects of a method that is essentially inartistic. With him, as with M. Zola, realism means the piling up of great masses of trivial fact, reporting in place of true characterization, and the enforcement of his argument by the bludgeon rather than by the rapier. Allowing for all that may be urged against the methods of railway companies in general, and in particular against the methods of the corporation that has held California within its constricting tentacles, we think that Mr. Norris has shown himself too evidently a partisan of the agriculturist, and has failed to deal impartially with the forces that

Reprinted from *Dial,* XXXI (September 1, 1901), 136.

contend for mastery in his pages. If only he had given the devil his due, we might be willing to admit the diabolic character of the corporation which he assails; as it is, we are rather inclined to sympathize with the octopus, which stands, after all, for practices that come within the form of law, whereas the practices of the wheat-growers stand for the most part without the law, and illustrate nearly every form of violence and anarchy. If the writer means to preach anything, it is that a certain degree of outrage justifies individuals in taking the law into their own hands, and this is the most dangerous sophistry that now confronts our civilization. We have little doubt, for example, that if Mr. Norris were writing of an earlier generation in California, he would be on the side of the Vigilance Committees rather than on the side of law and order. But his book is made an impressive one by virtue of its mere bulk and overwhelming particularity, as well as by certain dramatic episodes that are presented with remarkable vividness and intensity of feeling. And the vein of mysticism that crops out here and there is not only distinctly Zolaesque, but also provides a welcome relief from the oppressive atmosphere of the narrative. . . .

William Dean Howells

A Review of *The Octopus*

... "The Octopus" is an epic of Zolaesque largeness; but Mr. Norris is a poet of native note, and he owes to the great romantic realist nothing but the conception of treating a modern theme epically. . . . All that happens, happens around the oppression, ruthless, mechanical, increasing, of the land by the road, and the characters are the means direct and indirect of the infliction and affliction. They are not the less personalities because of their typical function; they are each most intimately and personally real, physically real, but also psychically real. . . .

. . . He gets back to something primitive, something primeval in his people; they love and hate with a sort of cave-dweller longing and loathing, yet with a modern environment of conscience that tells on them at last in fine despairs and remorses. The book has moments of drama which in the retrospect expand immensely, so that the afternoon of the rabbit-hunt and the evictions and the fight of the embattled farmers with the legal agents of the road seem a vast, wretched epoch of one's own. The stir of dumb cosmic forces is felt through all, but these are, if anything, a little too

Reprinted from *Harper's Monthly Magazine*, CIII (October 1901), 824-825.

invited, though their presence is of great imaginational conse-
quence. Certain episodes, loosely or not at all related to the main
purpose, we would prefer to have another time rather than lose
altogether. For the most part the story is compactly and strongly
built; it stands firmly, and it marches to the end with an awful,
automatic, inexorable trend, like a piece of relentless mechanism
endowed with organic activity. But the end is the fall of the great
leader of the farmers, who perishes morally and spiritually because
he has consented to employ the bad means of the road for the good
aims of the land; it is not the death of the road's local manager,
choked, drowned, buried in the avalanche of wheat which he has
robbed from the farmers. That is a bit of the melodrama towards
which Mr. Norris dangerously tends in his hours of triumphs.
Other defects his book has, but with them all it is a great book,
simple, sombre, large, and of a final authority as the record of a
tragical passage of American, of human events, which, if we did
not stand in their every-day presence, we should shudder at as the
presage of unexampled tyrannies. . . .

Anonymous

The Octopus

... 'The Octopus' is not a fully formed work; it has not lain quite long enough in the mental womb of its inception. Thus the critic, if he cared to dwell upon such things, could point out instances of over-fluency, the tautology which springs from uncooled enthusiasm, lack of restraint, and a verbosity which has robbed certain passages of the dignity belonging of right to the situations they describe. The girl Angelé Varian, for instance, is hardly once mentioned in these pages (and mention of her is not infrequent) without the phrase, "Her wide forehead made three-cornered by her plaits of gold hair." Regarding a statement upon p. 126, one would like to ask Mr. Norris whether even in America it is really possible that a horse can be shod in five minutes. "The leviathan with tentacles of steel clutching into the soil, the soulless Force, the iron-hearted Power, the Monster, the Colossus, the Octopus." The author may safely leave such laboured piling of effect to weaker men, whose work, lacking the body of his, demands more of stucco and paint. We note a tendency toward the flamboyant which Mr. Norris will have time to get well in hand and under

Reprinted from *The Athenaeum*, No. 3858, October 5, 1910, 447-448.

control before setting about the completion of his trilogy. In this and similar matters his work will derive great benefit from a stern and consistent use of the curb. The fifth chapter of 'The Octopus' is a long and strong chapter of fifty pages. It was a most unfortunate blunder to weaken and encumber it by closing upon two rushing pages of *résumé* of all that had gone before. All these blemishes are on the generous, opulent side, and have their root in the fact that the author is too close to the idea which possessed him. The critic points them out, but only with such kindly meant deprecation as that with which his comrades charge a gallant soldier with recklessness, and in the confident hope that the remaining two volumes in the wheat trilogy may be relieved of the handicap they involve.

'The Octopus' is a powerfully visualized picture of the evil wrought by great monopolies or "trusts." In this case the monopoly is a railway, its prey the wheat-growers and other producers in California. A list of the twenty-seven principal characters and a map of the district dealt with in the story form a serviceable frontispiece. The reviewer can recall no line of sentimentality in the book. Its handling of plain, elemental male characters, such as Magnus Derrick and Annixter (the best realized figure this), is consistent, strong, and altogether creditable. If it be true that it is not wisely described as an epic, it is equally true that it is a powerful and tragic piece of fiction.

H. W. Boynton

A Review of *The Octopus*

Mr. Norris's latest story is a more pretentious sort of work. It boasts a good deal of preliminary apparatus,—a note explaining that this is the first of a trilogy, duly billed as The Epic of the Wheat, a list of personæ, and a map of the region in which the action takes place. Photographs of a California wheat-field and a patent reaper and a tintype or two of the leading persons would have left still less for the imagination to do. But the author is a confessed realist, and his style, as well as his method, bears the Gallic hall-mark: "His smooth-shaven jowl stood out big and tremulous on either side of his face; the roll of fat on the nape of his neck, sprinkled with sparse, stiff hairs, bulged out with greater prominence. His great stomach, covered with a light brown linen vest, stamped with innumerable interlocked horseshoes, protruded far in advance, enormous, aggressive." This Mr. S. Behrman is eventually, in accordance with that poetic justice which even the realist cannot always resist, smothered to death in the hold of a wheat steamer. By that time the reader has learned so much about S. Behrman's person that (and this time the poetic justice reacts,

---

Reprinted from *Atlantic Monthly,* LXXXIX (May 1902), 708-9.

perhaps, against the story-teller) he is more pleased to be personally rid of an obnoxious animal than to have that story-world rid of the villain whose machinations have caused most of its troubles.

Hilma Tree we first know as a physically attractive animal, subtly colored after the manner of D'Annunzio's creatures: "Under her chin and under her ears the flesh was as white and smooth as floss satin, shading delicately to a faint delicate brown on her nape at the roots of her hair. Her throat rounded to meet her chin and cheek, with a soft swell of the skin, tinted pale amber in the shadows, but blending by barely perceptible gradations to the sweet warm flush of her cheek. The color on her temples was just touched with a certain blueness where the flesh was thin over the veining underneath. Her eyes were light brown . . . the lids—just a fraction of a shade darker than the hue of her face—were edged with lashes that were almost black." So much for the lust of the eye; presently we find the mystic Vanamee, many years after the death of his betrothed, recalling her in terms of another sense. He dwells habitually upon that "faint mingling of many oders, the smell of the roses that lingered in her hair, of the lilies that exhaled from her neck, of the heliotrope that disengaged itself from her hands and arms, and of the hyacinths of which her little feet were redolent." This is the sort of romantic vulgarity of which only the realist of the French school is capable. The world has pretty much stopped demanding that the Great American Novel shall be cast in an altogether new mould, but may still require it to be free from the method and manner of distinctly alien literatures. There are certain racial prescriptions of taste and style which cannot safely be ignored. Whatever is true of his manner, Mr. Norris's persons are certainly indigenous, and give the book its power. Presley and Vanamee one might have met elsewhere, but the Derricks, Annixter, and, above all, Hilma Tree,—what is the value to creative fiction of world-movements and commercial problems compared with such breathing human nature as this? . . .

B. O. Flower

The Trust in Fiction:
A Remarkable Social Novel

In "The Octopus," Mr. Norris has produced a novel of American life exhibiting the strength, power, vividness, fidelity to truth, photographic accuracy in description, and marvelous insight in depicting human nature, together with that broad and philosophic grasp of the larger problems of life, that noble passion for justice, that characterizes the greatest work of Emile Zola, without that sexualism or repulsive naturalism which the French writer so frequently forces upon his readers, and which is so revolting to the refined and healthy imagination.

"The Octopus" is a work so distinctly great that it justly entitles the author to rank among the very first American novelists. All the characters are real, living men and women, in whose veins runs the red blood of Nature. With one exception, each individual thinks, speaks, acts, and lives in harmony with the nature attributed to him. A noble consistency pervades the volume. Even individual inconsistencies are such as we all find in our own lives. The exception referred to is found in the pitiful sophistry accredited to the great railway magnate, Shelgrim, in which he seeks to shift from his head and the heads of the responsible directors, to the insensate railroad, the blame for the frightful and widespread ruin—the wanton slaughter of brave, loving, and industrious fathers, broth-

Reprinted from *Arena,* XXVII (May 1902), 547-554.

ers, and husbands, the destruction of once happy homes, the driving of men to crime and of women and girls to starvation and ruin— that was the direct result of calculating and premeditated deception and gross injustice, rendered possible only by bribery and wholesale corruption. When Shelgrim refers to the despoiling of the farmers of their homes, and to the death and ruin that had marked the recent tragedy, as due to the insensate railroad or to blind forces, and not to corrupt individuals, when he compares the railroad with the growing wheat, which unconsciously supplies the world with life-giving bread but is without responsibility for its beneficence, he not only insults the intelligence of the poet, but belittles himself in a way quite inconceivable by the utterance of such palpable sophistry. Nor is it imaginable that Presley, even though sick, distraught, and on the verge of nervous collapse, would for a moment have been impressed by such shallow twaddle and false similes. No; Shelgrim was no man to father such pitiful and absurdly fallacious reasoning before a free and intelligent man, though he doubtless did inspire precisely such utterances from the editors of his hireling press and the advocates paid by the railroad to retail such inane talk to voters too sodden and brutalized by long hours and hard toil to be able to see clearly or reason logically.

With this single exception the *dramatis personæ* of the volume think, speak, act, and live in exactly the way you and I, given similar characters, temperaments, and environment, would have thought and acted.

But "The Octopus" is far more than a strong, compelling, and virile story of American life: it is one of the most powerful and faithful social studies to be found in contemporaneous literature. It is a work that will not only stimulate thought: it will quicken the conscience and awaken the moral sensibilities of the reader. . . .

"The Octopus" is founded on a piece of actual history, stern, tragic, and ominous—the "Mussel Slough Affair"—in which the farmers of the San Joaquin Valley were dispossessed by the railroad company, and in their attempt to protect their roof-trees several persons were cruelly murdered. Though, perhaps, in some respects the author cannot be said to have painted the action of the railroad company as darkly as the cold facts of history would warrant, he has on the whole shadowed forth the central facts in a striking manner; while his marvelous descriptive power enables him to bring the case before the reader in so vivid a way that the scenes will long linger—gloomy and disquieting pictures—in memory's halls.

The dark deeds connected with Mussel Slough are typical of
many tragic passages that have marked the rise, onward march,
and domination of corporate greed—as, indeed, the story is thoroughly typical of the mighty struggle between the people and the
trusts. . . .

It remained for Mr. Norris, however, to present in a bold, striking, and powerful romance a concrete illustration, true in spirit,
method and detail, of the conflict that has been waged beween
the trusts and the people. . . .

"The Octopus" is a work of genius. Not only is it a powerful
romance of compelling interest—thrilling, dramatic, and so graphic
that its various shifting scenes stand out clear-cut and unforget-
table, but as a social study it possesses a historical value equaled
by few works of fiction. It is, broadly speaking, typically historical
not only of the great railroad corporation, whose story is so well
known on the Pacific Coast, but of the railroad corporations of the
United States, and of the trusts in general.

It is part of the settled policy of the complacent tools and ser-
vants of corporate power to seek to discredit all such pictures,
even though they know full well that for more than a quarter of a
century the baleful influence of corporate greed has been felt
throughout the length and breadth of the land, not only in the
levying of unjust tributes on the poor but in the debauching and
corruption of government in all its ramifications. "The Octopus"
shows in a vivid manner how this supreme tragedy—this lowering
of the political ideals from the fundamental demands of justice,
honesty, and freedom to subserviency to capitalistic aggression—
has been accomplished in the United States. It is very easy for
apologists and beneficiaries of corporate corruption to seek to
discredit such pictures as "fiction." The facts on which this novel
is based, however, were a terrible reality; and the methods by
which the great railroad power became well-nigh omnipotent on
the Pacific Coast have been indicated by the publication of letters of
C. P. Huntington to General Colton. These communications, it will
be remembered, were made public in the famous suit brought in
Santa Rosa, California, to decide whether the widow of General
Colton had been fairly dealt with by the railroad company, in
whose confidential service the General had long been engaged. In
these letters we have a startling revelation of how the railroad
magnates tampered with officials, how they made and unmade committees, how they worked in Congress through the press, how
neither Governors, Congressmen, statesmen, members of the Cabi-

net and judges, the Associated Press, nor the editors of the country escaped the argus eyes of the railroad officials. . . .

But it must not be imagined that "The Octopus" is primarily a social study. It is above all a great literary creation. The author is at all times the artist. Only on rare occasions, like the following for example, do the characters moralize. Here, however, we have the great California manufacturer, Cedarquist, thus referring to the supreme peril of the Republic:

"If I were to name the one crying evil of American life, . . . it would be the indifference of the better people to public affairs. It is so in all our great centers. There are other great trusts, God knows, in the United States, besides our own dear P. and S. W. Railroad. Every State has its own grievance. If it is not a railroad trust, it is a sugar trust, or an oil trust, or an industrial trust, that exploits the People, *because the People allow it.* The indifference of the People is the opportunity of the despot. It is as true as that the whole is greater than a part, and the maxim is so old that it is trite—it is laughable. It is neglected and disused for the sake of some new ingenious and complicated theory, some wonderful scheme of re-organization, but the fact remains, nevertheless, simple, fundamental, everlasting. The People have but to say 'No,' and not the strongest tyranny, political, religious, or financial, that was ever organized could survive one week."

Mr. Norris unfolds a mighty drama, which concerns our own time. He paints colossal pictures so vividly that there is small need for didactic moralizing about them. One feels from the first that he is in the presence of a great artist, a man of real genius; and though there is more of shadow than of sunshine in the highly dramatic romance there are many passages of great beauty. The descriptions of Nature and her marvelous works, the portraying of Vanamee, and the wonderful transformation of Annixter are typical examples of the beauty and poetry that abound in this volume.

"The Octopus" is a novel that every reader of THE ARENA should possess. If it is impossible for you to procure more than one work of fiction this season, my advice—my unhesitating advice—is to buy "The Octopus," read it aloud to your family, and then lend it to your neighbors. In so doing you will be helping to awaken the people from the death-dealing slumber that has been brought about by the multitudinous influences of corporate greed, controlling the machinery of government and the opinion-forming agencies of the Republic.

3. Criticism and Scholarship

Franklin Walker

From
Frank Norris: A Biography

After his material was in hand, Norris spent a full year in writing *The Octopus*. In working on his earlier novels he had been guided by the evolution of the story, but now he assumed the attitude of a research worker, carefully planning his work beforehand. He wrote plot summaries, he worked out an "index sheet" for each character, he tabulated and arranged his notes, he made a map of the country where his action was to take place. He played the game of organization with zest, pleased with the formidable piles of notes, gleefully enthusiastic about the map. He went about his work methodically and scientifically, for he was writing "a novel with a purpose."

... *The Octopus*, as Norris worked it out, did lend itself to a propagandic interpretation, which was furthered by a misreading of the novel on the part of a public which asked for an attack on the railroads. However, *The Octopus* was not written to reveal the injustice of the railroads or to attack the control of the trusts. We have seen that Norris approached it as an integral part of the epic of the wheat and selected the railroad-farmer issue because it promised him the most drama. His purpose in *The Octopus* was to reveal the working of economic forces, to portray the clash between producer and distributor, and to picture a segment of American civilization. It is very probable that his personal attitude toward the central conflict agreed more completely with Shelgrim's than with Presley's; he had far more in common with the employer than with the anarchist. His failure in his intention of presenting the conflict objectively, in stating both sides of the issue, was not the result of a social theory but of a love for stupendous action. Once he considered the railroad as an octopus, crushing out the lives of those whom it reached with its tentacles, the dramatic possibilities piled up; as he discovered injustice after injustice in the California records, he added them to the story to strengthen his climax. The railroad must be made as powerful as possible in order to put up a good fight. It is once more the apotheosis of force.

With his general conception in mind, Norris next turned his attention to his characters . . . . he made a list of the principal characters of the novel, some thirty in number . . . . For each person in the novel, Norris prepared a character sketch which included notes on the physical appearance, the personality, whatever symbolic value there might be, and the labeling phrases which he intended to repeat, like Homeric refrains, whenever the character appeared in the story. A sheaf of notes remains to illustrate his method; thus we known Annixter before the novel was begun. "P.s. 13-14-15. Annixter. A male cast of countenance. The jaw heavy, the lower lip thrust out. The chin masculine and deeply cleft . . . Stiff yellow hair, always in disorder. A little tuft of it always standing out from his crown like a feather on an Indian's scalp.— Continually seeking an argument. 'In a way it is and then again in a way it isn't.' David Copperfield. His stomach—eats *dried prunes*. A ferocious worker. Extremely inconsistent. Obstinate, contrary, dictatorial, wilful, perverse. Great executive ability. Very shrewd, far-sighted, suspicious. Admiration for Presley. The two great friends. Accepts no direct statement with modification—*a woman hater. Contradicts everything. 'Fool feemale girls'* to take up a man's time. Suspicious that all women are 'trying to get hold on him.' Fear of involving himself in a petticoat mess. Clumsy when women are about. Talks about his 'nature' and his stomach. His worst insult is to call a man *a Pip*. Spits with wonderful ac-

curacy. 'Whit.' Hates Derrick's cat. Belligerent, truculent, turbu-
lent, irascible. 'Hooks, nails and fetters,' 'Horse, foot, and dragoon,'
'lock, stock, and barrel'."[1]

As Norris worked on his *dramatis personœ*, he furthered his
realistic aim by using his acquaintances as prototypes for characters. . . .

In one instance at least, Norris thought of his characters first
as symbols rather than types or individuals. This confusion of
methods explains the presence of Angéle Varian and to some extent
Vanamee. His notes on Angéle state that she is to be "a contrast
with Hilma. The Embodiment of Night—pallid gold and pale car-
nation. She is the symbol of the wheat." Under Hilma Tree:
"Contrast Hilma and Angéle. Hilma is always seen in the sun.
Angéle at night under the moon. One hale, honest, radiant. The
other mysterious, troublous, perplexing. Hilma is the embodiment
of day." Angéle is to die, leaving a daughter who is to appear to
Vanamee on the same night in which the wheat comes up. The
effect is to be heightened by the blossoming of the flowers in the
seed garden. With the return of Angéle in the form of her daughter,
the grave will be vanquished. "Life out of death, eternity rising
from out of dissolution. Angéle was not the symbol but the proof
of immortality." So with the fecundity of the earth, with the
wheat, with all creation. . . . Angéle is to be drawn from the flower
bed by Vanamee's will power. Here Norris planned to use a subject
which had long fascinated him. He had listened to Bruce Porter
discuss mysticism, hypnotism, thought transference. He had been
impressed by Du Maurier's use of Svengali's power in *Trilby*. He
had endowed McTeague with a sixth sense, an intuitive awareness
of danger. Now, again, he planned to exploit an unnatural sense
in a dramatic manner, giving to Vanamee the power of attracting
others by thought transference. It would be another power, the
force of will, symbolic of the force which brought the wheat to the
surface. Finally, the Vanamee-Angéle incidents would furnish an
idyllic element to contrast with the stark tragedy. Once more
Norris attempted to create one extreme to balance another; it was
to be one of the major mistakes of the book, an extraneous and
formless blur on the canvas, the most indigestible portion of the
ragout. . . . The fight by the ranchers was effective, the downfall
of Magnus Derrick was effective; but the movement carried on

---

[1]Letter to Isaac Marcosson, dated November 15, 1899. *Adventures in Inter-
viewing,* N.Y.: John Lane, 1919, p. 236.

beyond the melodramatic pathos of Mrs. Hooven starving on the streets of San Francisco while railroad barons ate ortolan patties and discussed art, to end with a final hollow crash in the stifling of the arch villain, S. Behrman, beneath a deluge of wheat—a melodramatic conclusion rivaled only in the works of Dickens and Hugo. . . . In September, 1900, Norris reviewed his labors: "The Squid is nearing conclusion. Hooray! I can see the end. It is the hardest work I ever have done in my life, a solid year of writing and four months' preparation—bar two months—and *I* think the best thing far and away I ever did. You've no idea of the outside work on it. I've been in correspondence with all kinds of people during its composition, from the Traffic Manager of a Western railroad to the sub-deputy-assistant of the Secretary of Agriculture at Washington. Also in connection with it all I've helped run and work a harvester in the San Joaquin—that is, I've helped on the sacking platform—but of course you don't know where that is. Well, the thing is mostly done now and I know when it slumps and I know when it strikes and I think the strikes are the most numerous and important. I know that in the masses I've made no mistake. You will find some things in it that—for me—are new departures. It is the most romantic thing I've ever done. One of the secondary sub-plots is pure romance—oh, even mysticism, if you like, a sort of allegory—I call it the allegorical side of the wheat subject—and the fire in it is the Allegory of the Wheat. . . ."[1]

On December 15, 1900, Norris finished *The Octopus* and delivered it to the publishers. When it appeared the following April, it was to mark several milestones in American fiction; it was to be the first of a long stream of novels dealing broadly with economic currents in American life, it was to make the first noteworthy stride towards the fiction of the Western frontier, and, through its vigor and breadth, it was to make still another inroad upon the hold of sentimental and petty fiction, offering a model of substance to the younger writers who were to carry on.

Granville Hicks

From *The Great Tradition*

Though the second volume, *The Pit*, falls far below Norris' conception, the first, *The Octopus*, is not wholly unworthy of the name of epic. Woven out of a dozen strands, it achieves the dimensions necessary for the adequate portrayal of a great economic struggle. It depicts a movement by depicting people, scores of them, all caught up in the battle between the wheat-raisers and the railroad. On page after page, in analyses of character, in descriptions of ranchers' meetings, of wheat fields, of fighting, Norris gives us the substance of a struggle that, in its fundamentals, was nationwide. He had at least one quality of greatness: he could seize upon the central issues of his time and create people in whose lives those issues were reflected.

Yet *The Octopus* can scarcely be called a great book; it is too confused, and in the end too false. Norris' growing sympathy with the people made him sorry for the dispossessed ranchers, and he could even become indignant at their misfortunes. But on the other hand, he admired the romantic boldness of Collis P. Huntington,

Reprinted from *The Great Tradition* (New York: The Macmillan Company, 1933), 168-175, by permission of the author.

who appears in the book under the name of Shelgrim. Moreover, he had talked with Huntington, as Presley talks with Shelgrim, and he could see no flaw in the railroad president's argument that the way of the railroad was the way of progress. Somehow he had to reconcile these conflicting sympathies if he was to make his novel an interpretation of life. His reading of Zola had introduced him to determinism, which he had empolyed as a literary device in both *McTeague* and *Vandover and the Brute*, though he seems never to have understood its philosophic implications. And a deterministic version of the apologies of the captains of industry, as stated in Shelgrim's interview with Presley, provided him with his method of interpretation. One recalls Presley's meditations at the end of the book: "Men—motes in the sunshine—perished, were shot down in the very noon of life, hearts were broken, little children were started in life lamentably handicapped; young girls were brought to a life of shame; old women died in the heart of life for lack of food. . . . *But the WHEAT remained.* Untouched, unassailable, undefiled, that mighty world-force, that nourisher of nation, wrapped in Nirvanic calm, indifferent to the human swarm, gigantic, resistless, moved onward in its appointed grooves . . . . Falseness dies; injustice and oppression in the end of everything fade away. Greed, cruelty, selfishness, and inhumanity are short-lived; the individual suffers, but the race goes on. . . . The larger view always and through all shams, all wickedness, discovers the Truth that will, in the end, prevail, and all things, surely, inevitably, resistlessly work together for good."

This is consoling doctrine, and no doubt it seemed to Norris to answer his purposes. The thoughtful reader, however, finds Presley's rhapsody the most disturbing kind of anticlimax. As a theory it is ridiculous, and it destroys the emotional effect of the book, for it means that the contemptible Behrman has worked as surely for good as the noble Derrick, the impulsive Annixter, or the violent Dyke. Moreover, the consequences of this philosophy are found on page after page. How many problems Norris leaves unsolved: Magnus Derrick's ethical dilemma, the whole question of the use of violence, the place of the poet in such a struggle as that between the railroad and the ranchers! And how far he is from a consistent interpretation of character! For example, in interpreting Magnus' downfall he wavers between the view that his surrender is ignoble and the view that it is inevitable. Presley hovers on the edge of the struggle, now repelled, now drawn in, and at last takes refuge in his mystical optimism. The confusion permeates even the minutiæ of the book: we are asked to believe that Vanamee has a sixth sense, that Annixter is capable of a miraculous transformation under the influence of pure love. Norris' old romanticism creeps in again and again, sheltered by the incoherence of his philosophy. Even the method is confused, for austere realism often yields to overt melodrama and careful objectivity to special pleading.

H. Willard Reninger

Norris Explains
The Octopus: A Correlation
of His Theory and Practice

Before the appearance of Granville Hick's *The Great Tradition* in 1933, the historians and critics of the American novel seemed not to have found any inconsistency or confusion in Frank Norris's novel, *The Octopus* (1901). Mr. Hicks, however, is quite sure that Norris "seems never to have understood . . . [the] philosophic implications" of determinism "which he had employed as a literary device in both *McTeague* and *Vandover and the Brute*. . . ." Norris's misunderstanding, continues Mr. Hicks, is apparent in his attempt in *The Octopus* to reconcile determination with the large view that all things inevitably work together for good.[1] Since the publication of Mr. Hick's study, however, other critics have also found it difficult to interpret *The Octopus* without discovering Norris's philosophical confusion.

Although Parrington and Hartwick and Pattee and Blankenship —all writing before 1933—had not observed this alleged confusion in Norris, two others, writing after 1933, have found Mr. Hicks to be quite right. Professor W. F. Taylor has learned that "Norris

Reprinted from *American Literaure,* XII (May, 1940), 218-27, by permission of Duke University Press.
[1]*The Great Tradition,* (rev. ed.; New York, 1935), pp. 172-173.

goes halting between the contradictory opinions of determinism and moral order" in *The Octopus*,[2] and Dr. Charles Walcutt finds the confusion "a shocking one," although he can curiously conclude that "in the last analysis *The Octopus* is one of the finest American novels written before 1910."[3] Professor A. H. Quinn, however, in his recent study of American fiction is silent on this charge of confusion in Norris.[4]

I am struck with the fact that none of these critics, especially the derogatory ones, has taken the trouble to collate *The Octopus* with Norris's own literary theory as we find it in *The Responsibilities of the Novelist* (1903); and I strongly surmise that a correlative study of these books will demonstrate the weakness in Mr. Hick's position. I suspect, in fact, that too little is known concerning Norris's objectives while he was writing *The Octopus;* and this suspicion is somewhat fortified when I find Carl Van Doren saying that *"The Responsibilities of the Novelist*...shows... [Norris] to have been less a thinker than a passionate partisan of the rising doctrine of naturalism,"[5] and Professors Howard Mumford Jones and Ernest E. Leisy saying that *"The Responsibilities of the Novelist* became the pronunciamento of the new school" of naturalism.[6] A thorough reading of *The Responsibilities* will reveal that Norris was actually attacking "that harsh, loveless, colorless, blunt tool" called naturalism.

The purpose of this paper, therefore, is to permit Norris to explain his own novel by applying the literary theory in *The Responsibilities* to *The Octopus*. Before proceeding to such an explanation, however, it will be necessary first to state the few biographical facts related to the changes in Norris's theory and practice before *The Octopus* was written.

I

In 1887, when Frank Norris was seventeen years old, he was taken by his parents to Europe, where he attended an art school in Paris. Although he was in the very home of naturalism, "he passed the stalls filled with Balzac, Flaubert, and Zola, the proper food

[2] *A History of American Letters* (New York, 1936), p. 314.
[3] "Naturalism in the American Novel" (unpublished University of Michigan thesis, 1937), pp. 340-342.
[4] *American Fiction: An Historical and Critical Survey* (New York, 1936), pp. 627-628.
[5] *The American Novel* (New York, 1921), p. 264.
[6] *Major American Writers* (New York, 1935), p. 1501.

for one who was to become a naturalist, and plunged unhesitatingly into the romantic Middle Ages. It was not Zola's L'Assommoir nor Flaubert's *Madame Bovary* which won his heart, but Froissart's Chronicles."[7]

A year later, his interest began to turn from art to writing, and this writing emerged from his enthusiasm for the fourteenth century. But after having matriculated in the University of California in 1890, he confessed to a growing conviction that "an hour's experience is worth ten years of study."[8] Although he had neglected Zola while he was in Paris, he now "started an ambitious program of novel-writing under the spur of Zola," beginning *McTeague* in his senior year (1894). Leaving the University of California without having taken a degree, he went to Harvard during 1894-1895 to study with Professor Lewis E. Gates, under whom he wrote much of *Vandover and the Brute* and *McTeague*, two pieces of uncompromising naturalism. Although *Vandover* was not published until 1914, Norris went into the Sierras at the Big Dipper Mine in October, 1897, in order to finish *McTeague*, which was published in the spring of 1899. It is significant, however, that during the very years he was writing and publishing *McTeague*, he was also writing an "idyllic autobiography," *Blix* (1899), another romance entitled *Moran of the Lady Letty* (1898), and a story of love and arctic exploration called *A Man's Woman* (1900). In his enthusiasm for his first success in *McTeague* he began *The Octopus*, the first book of a projected trilogy, which was finished December 15, 1900, and published in April, 1901. Immediately after the appearance of *The Octopus*, Norris, whose fame was spreading fast, was requested by various magazines to state his ideas on literary theory and life; he responded with a series of essays written in 1901-1902, which finally became *The Responsibilities* a year after his death in 1902.

Out of these biographical facts[9] emerge a number of signficant conclusions. Norris had begun his career as a romantic, but later became a disciple of Zola, and wrote *Vandover* and *McTeague*. He then published *Moran*, a romance, followed by *The Octopus*, and concluded his career, with the exception of *The Pit* (1902), with *The Responsibilities* which, despite the statement of Carl Van Doren, I hope to show is an attack on, not a defense of, naturalism. The chronology clearly indicates that during the last four years of

---

[7]Franklin Walker, *Frank Norris: A Biography* (Garden City, N.Y., 1932), p. 33.
[8]Quoted in *ibid.*, p. 51.
[9]*Ibid.*, chaps. ii-xii, *passim.*

his life Norris was definitely leaving the pessimistic naturalism of Zola and was turning to a theory and practice of his own. The nature of these we are now in a position to examine.

II

Norris's biographer says that *The Responsibilities* "contains Norris's declaration of faith."[10] Although very little historical or critical interpretation has been rendered this declaration of faith, I am convinced that it is a far more penetrating volume than any student of American criticism has yet revealed.[11] Norris's theory of the novel can be best approached through an understanding of what he was protesting against in contemporaneous literary theory.

The essays which now constitute *The Responsibilities* were written in 1901-1902, while at least three theories of the novel were urging their own claims for supremacy; (1) that of romance which dealt with the remote, the wonderful, and the should-be; (2) that of Howells which glorified the commonplace, the simple, the natural, and the honest; and (3) that of the French naturalists. It is chiefly because Norris found each of these theories[12] inadequate that he wrote his essays of protest and constructed a theory of the novel of his own.

Norris's theory of the novel flows logically from three postulates. First, since the people now look to the novelist with confidence, he must above all approach life and his art with uncompromising sincerity—an approach closely akin to Garland's "candor," and James's "seriousness." The novelist must courageously investigate all conditions in actual life, and then embody his interpretation of

---

[10]*Ibid.,* p. 289.
[11]Note, for example, the treatment given Norris in George E. De Mille's *Literary Criticism in America* (New York, 1931), pp. 198-202. After having admitted that "Norris's main contribution to the theory of the novel, has not had, I think, the attention it deserves," Mr. De Mille renders him the compliment of little more than three pages, although Stedman is given twenty-four. To indicate the nature of one of Norris's finest contributions to American critical theory, the distinction between romance and realism, Mr. De Mille quotes thirty-two words from *The Responsibilities* which are among the most insignificant of Norris's entire book, and then comments, "The trouble with a definition of that kind is that it makes no distinctions." Mr. De Mille might have said that "the trouble with Norris's distinctions is that they cannot be reduced to simple definitions."
[12]For an extended examination of these three theories see my "Theory and Practice of the American Novel, 1867-1903" (unpublished University of Michigan thesis, 1938), pp. 229-374.

the facts of existence in his art. "The attitude of the novelist toward his fellow men and women," wrote Norris, "is the great thing, not his inventiveness, his ingenuity, his deftness, or glibness, or verbal dexterity."[13] Second, the novelist must have the power of penetrating beneath the clothes of men, and beyond both to the heart of man. This second postulate is closely related to the point of view in Carlyle's *Sartor Resartus* insofar as both men believed that all "clothes," forms, and human institutions are but temporary symbols of the eternally living man which must be penetrated in order to find him.[14] We therefore find Norris insisting that the novel "must penetrate deep into the motives and character of type men, men who are composite pictures of a multitude of men."[15] And third, Norris held that the novelist is organically constituted so as to make it necessary for him to *select* his material, to *arrange* it psychologically (not necessarily logically as it appears in actual life for any given twenty-four hours), and to "prove something, [to] draw conclusions from a whole congeries of forces, social tendencies, race impulses, [and to] devote himself not to a study of men but of man."[16] To select, to arrange, and to prove: these are the distinguishing abilities of the true novelist. From these three postulates Norris derives his theory of genuine realism, or, if you like, genuine romance.[17]

Genuine realism, argues Norris, is not one "of mere externals" but rather one "of motives and emotions." This distinction is one

[13]*The Responsibilities of the Novelist* (Garden City, N.Y., 1928), p. 218.

[14]". . . the one idea of the fakir—the copyist—and of the public which for the moment listens to him, is Clothes . . . Not Clothes only in the sense of doublet and gown, but Clothes of speech, Clothes of manner, Clothes of customs . . . Do these Little People [those who read the fakirs] know that Scott's archeology was about one thousand years 'out' in *Ivanhoe* . . .? But is it not . . . Ivanhoe [that we want], not his clothes, his armour? And in spite of his errors Scott gave us a real Ivanhoe. He got beneath the clothes of an epoch and got the heart of it and the spirit of it . . . and he put forth a masterpiece" (*ibid.*, p. 14).

[15]*Ibid.*, p. 22.

[16]*Loc. cit.* Franklin Walker observes that in Norris's "eyes the novel with a purpose did not attempt to manipulate a story to prove a theory but rather attempted to present the evidence from which theories could be deduced" (*op. cit.*, p. 254).

[17]*Genuine Realism* and *genuine romance* are precisely the same things to Norris; they meant for him genuine truth. He uses the terms *romance* and *realism* merely because they were found in the critical terminology of his time, not because he believes they have any standardized meaning. In fact, he is actually dismissing these terms and defining the genuine novelist who deals with genuine truth.

between physical realism and psychological realism, or the difference between external actuality and internal reality. "The difficult
thing," says Norris,

> is to get at the life immediately around you—the very life in which
> you move. No romance in it? No romance in *you,* poor fool. As
> much romance on Michigan Avenue [Chicago] as there is realism
> in King Arthur's court. *It is as you choose to see it.* The important
> thing to decide is, which formula is the best to help you grip the
> Real Life of this or any other age. . . . Romance and realism are
> constant qualities of every age, day, and hour. . . . They will con-
> tinue to exist till the end of time, *not so much in the things as in
> point of view of the people who see things.*[18]

The problem, then, resolves itself to the question, what kind of eyes
will you look with? One can *see* actuality, but one can only *perceive*
reality. To know this reality, says Norris,

> you must live—if not *among* people, then *in* people. You must be
> something more than a novelist if you can, something more than
> just a writer. There must be that nameless sixth sense or sensibility
> in you that great musicians have in common with great inventors
> and great scientists. . . . It is not genius, for genius is a lax, loose
> term so flippantly used that its expressiveness is long since lost. It
> is more akin to sincerity.[19]

With such a concept of romantic-reality Norris dismissed (1)
pseudo-romance, "the cut-and-thrust stories"; (2) "that harsh,
loveless, colorless, blunt tool" of naturalism; and (3) that fiction as
"respectable as a church and proper as a deacon—as, for instance,
the novels of Mr. Howells." The proper substitute, says Norris, is
"an instrument keen, finely tempered, flawless—an instrument
with which we may go straight through the clothes and tissues
and wrapping of flesh down deep into the red, living heart of
things.[20] Such an instrument will search "the unplumbed depths of
the human heart, and the mystery of sex, and the problems of life,
and the blacks, unsearched penetralia of the soul of man."[21]

Identified with this concept of finding reality by going beyond
actuality is Norris's concept of idealized realism, a method which

---

[18]*The Responsibilities,* p. 16. Italics mine, except for the single word *you.*
[19]*Ibid.,* p. 17. Norris's italics.
[20]*Ibid.,* p. 163.
[21]*Ibid.,* pp. 167-168.

produces something closely akin to Aristotle's ideal truth, or the superiority of probable impossibility over possible improbability. Norris sums up his own concept of imitation:

> In the fine arts we do not care one little bit about what life actually is, but what it looks like to an interesting impressionable man, and if he tells his story or paints his picture so that the majority of intelligent people wil say, "Yes, that must have been just about what would have happened under those circumstances," he is true. His accuracy cuts no figure at all. *He need not be accurate if he does not choose to be. If he sees fit to be inaccurate in order to make his point—so only his point be the conveying of a truthful impression—that is his affair.*[22]

What is this but a statement of the Aristotelian paradox which permits an artist to be false to the actual in order to be true to the general? This principle leads us to a consideration of Norris's philosophy of structure.

Like James and Stevenson, Norris thought no apology necessary for directing serious attention to the basic mechanics of the novel. He recognizes that

> in all human occupations, trades, arts or business, science, morals or religion, there exists, way at the bottom, a homogeneity and a certain family likeness so that, quite possibly after all, the discussion of the importance of the mechanics of fiction may be something more than mere speculative sophistry.[23]

As Aristotle said of tragedy, Norris argues that an extended piece of fiction must have

> a beginning and an end, which implies a middle, continuity, which implies movement, which in turn implies a greater speed or less, an accelerated, retarded or broken action . . .; [for] no one who sets a thing in motion but keeps an eye and a hand upon its speed.[24]

A novel, Norris is saying, must be architecturally constructed, resulting in a moving organic whole. This growing organism, under the cautious eye and hand of the artist, moves on to

> the pivotal event, . . . the peg upon which the fabric of the [whole novel] . . . hangs, the nucleus around which the shifting drifts and

---

[22]*Ibid.,* p. 173. Italics mine.
[23]*Ibid.,* p. 113.
[24]*Loc. cit.*

currents must—suddenly—coagulate, the sudden releasing of the brake to permit for one instant the entire machinery to labour, full steam, ahead. Up to that point the action must lead; from it, it must decline.[25]

To show precisely how the novelist *causes* this to happen Norris traces the building of the organic whole in minute detail, indicating how the novelist arrives at the pivotal event, when

in a twinkling the complication is solved with all the violence of an explosion, and the catastrophe, the climax, the pivotal event fairly leaps from the pages with a rush of action that leaves you stunned, breathless, and overwhelmed with the sheer power of its presentation. And there is a master work of fiction.[26]

Since the chapters, too, are to be built upon the same plan, the series of pictures produced by them, organically related, finally leads to the pivotal event. But, as if to warn us that this pivotal event must not merely be thrown in for purposes of excitement and thrill, Norris points out that "it is the context of the story that makes . . . [the pivotal event] so tremendous . . .; [it is] *prepared for . . . from the novel's initial chapter.*"[27]

Summarized, Norris's theory of novel construction may be put in this way: Postulating a necessary dramatic effect, the novelist must consciously build a novel with a beginning and an end which imply a middle, and continuity which implies movement, the height of which arrives with the pivotal event. Each chapter, in order to facilitate this movement, is itself, in little, built on the same plan, except that its time is continuous and its environment unchanged. Such chapters, therefore, organically join themselves for the express purpose of permitting, finally, the events of the novel to culminate within the consciousness of the reader as a single dramatic effect.[28]

Fortified, now, with Norris's own theory of realism and his theory of novel construction, we are prepared to interpret *The Octopus*.

III

The Octopus stands more or less as the climax of American sociological realism after the Civil War as *The Responsibilities*

[25]*Ibid.*, p. 114.
[26]*Ibid.*, p. 115.
[27]*Ibid.*, p. 116. Italics mine.
[28]This theory, of course, is Poe's classical theory of the short story further refined for the purposes of the novel.

stands as the climax of American critical theory of the novel in the nineteenth century.[29] The latter was written immediately after the former, and each is complementary to the other even in minute detail; consequently, *The Octopus* is a rather complete illustration of the theory found in *The Responsibilities*.

We have seen above that Norris has argued that a great novel must prove something by "drawing conclusions from a whole congeries of forces, social tendencies, race impulses, [by] devoting itself not to a study of men but of man."[30]

Interpreting this statement with our knowledge of Norris's theory of novel construction, we then understand that the novel is to be so constructed in Aristotelian fashion that an ideal philosophical truth shall finally emerge from its totality. We are therefore pressed to answer the obvious question, What does *The Octopus* prove?

The novel dramatizes the doctrine that although men in a given locality can be temporarily defeated by combined economic and political forces, which in themselves are temporary and contingent on a phase of a civilization, the *natural* forces, epitomized by the wheat, which are eternal and resistless, will eventually bring about the greatest good for the greatest number. It is this doctrine which reconciles the alleged inconsistencies in the novel. Hence, when Shelgrim tells Presley that forces, not men, control the wheat,[31] he unquestionably voices a deterministic doctrine, *but Shelgrim has by no means told the whole story*. The conclusion of the whole matter is voiced by Vanamee who has been endowed with this sixth sense which Norris has made the cardinal faculty of the novelist. The mystical Vanamee tells Presley:

> "We shall probably never meet again . . . but if these are the last words I ever speak to you, listen to them, and remember them, because I know I speak the truth. Evil is short-lived. Never judge of the whole round of life by the mere segment you can see. The whole is, in the end, perfect."[32]

These words, when correlated with the last two pages of the novel which are concluded with the idea that "the Truth . . . will, in the end, prevail, and all things, surely, inevitably, resistlessly [will] work together for good," unquestionably represent Norris's ideal philosophical truth which he has "drawn from a whole congeries

---

[29]See my "Theory and Practice of the American Novel, 1867-1903," chap. iv.
[30]*The Responsibilities*, p. 22.
[31]*The Octopus* (Garden City, N.Y., 1928), II, 285.
[32]*Ibid.*, II, 345.

of forces." And, to be sure, the truth is deterministic, not in the direction of naturalistic evil as in *McTeague* or *Vandover*, but rather in the direction of inevitable good.

It is very significant that Vanamee, the mystic, teaches Presley, the socialist-poet of the great struggle, the lesson to be found in the resistless flow of the wheat. Whether Norris believed in the mystical method of gathering truth is irrelevant to his conclusion, for Vanamee's mysticism is merely a technique used by Norris to get at "the larger view" of things: Vanamee is the only character in the novel whose temperamental equipment (his "sixth sense") permits him to look far enough into the future in order to perceive that the struggle and temporary defeat of the men *directly* involved are only segments of the whole.

The method by which Norris caused this romantic-realistic doctrine of the inevitable good to "leap" (as he said) from his pages can be described as follows. Since the novel treats of the struggle between the ranchers and the railroad and the social consequences involved, Norris presents in the first chapter a conversation between Presley and Harran Derrick in which Harran complains that the ranchers have lost their rate-case to the railroad. He exclaims bitterly, "Why not hold us up with a gun in our faces. . . ?" (p. 9). Only six pages later Dyke describes his unfair treatment by the railroad; and before the action is well started the locomotive, the Octopus, kills the sheep, an act which is obviously symbolical of the future fate of the people in the valley. In the first fifty pages, therefore, we understand the unjust power employed by the Octopus, the various ways in which it is used, the various types of people who suffer because of its tyranny, and the extent to which this injustice can be applied before the victims will begin to fight back. All this is Norris's "beginning."

The "middle" is a moving organism which integrates a culminating series of dramas, each drama, growing logically (or psychologically, which is more important always to Norris) from its predecessors, in which the struggle is intensified because the emotional reaction of these men to the increasing injustice develops in direct proportion to the weight of the impending tragedy involved. The pivotal event is Behrman's being drowned in his own unjustly-acquired wheat as it pours into the hold of the ship; and the truth —asked for by Norris—which "leaps" from the "end" of the action is that in the long run truth will prevail—briefly, whatever is, is right.

In *The Octopus*, then, Norris has given the truth as he sees it concerning (1) the immediate struggle between men and the railroad, and (2) the philosophical implications arising from the struggle of men against the elemental forces. He has shown us what lies beneath the clothes of men, and the nature of the heart of emotional desires of men. And he has selected and arranged the materials of these struggles in order to deduce from them their intrinsic meaning. Having done these things he has avoided pseudo-romance, commonplace realism, and pessimistic naturalism, giving us instead an example of his own concept of romantic-reality. Apparently, then, *The Octopus* does not miss greatness because of its confusion; rather, its greatness is heightened because of the novel's philosophical consistency.

Ernest Marchand

From *Frank Norris:*
A Study

One item . . . among the probable influences that made *The Octopus* a contribution to the literature of social justice, seems certain: Norris was much impressed by Edwin Markham's *The Man with the Hoe*. The astounding success of Markham's poem (first published in the *San Francisco Examiner*, January 15, 1899) is one of the noteworthy incidents in the literary history of the 'nineties. Without disparagement to *The Man with the Hoe*, it is hardly conceivable that it would meet with similar acclaim today. It arrived at the precise moment fitted to receive it. It seemed to crystallize the long-gathering exasperation and sense of wrong of a whole people beginning to feel that something had gone awry with the fine promise of its democracy; beginning to feel the weight and pressure of the industrial-financial order that had been gathering its powers during the preceding four decades; beginning to understand, as Norris put it, that "an evil tree was growing in the midst of the garden." Presley's poem, "The Toilers," in its inspiration by a celebrated French painting, in its first appearance in a daily newspaper, and in the storm of praise, ridicule, and abuse which it raised, offers an exact parallel to the history of *The Man with the Hoe*.

In *The Octopus* the issue is squarely joined: it is organized wealth against the people. It is Presley who is charged with the responsibility of bearing Norris' "message." Presley views the whole drama of the struggle with the octopus, from the first sly stirring of the monster's tentacles to the final relentless contortion with which it destroys its last victim. He is present at every crisis, witnesses all the agonies, suffers them all vicariously, burns with indignation, and emerges at last, solitary, ineffectual, a dreamer, consoling himself with the thought that the wheat is on its way to feed the starving scarecrows of India and that good can never die —though he has seen it rather roughly handled. But if he is the vehicle of the author's emotions and ideas, Norris maintains toward him at the same time a certain detachment, freely revealing his weaknesses, his confusion of thought, his moral bewilderment. Always Norris strives to keep to what he calls "the larger view," to embrace within his scheme of great impersonal forces both oppressors and oppressed.

In the alignment, however, of his opposing powers, he shows a faulty analysis. The People (always spelled with a capital letter) are represented by the ranchers of the San Joaquin. Who are these men? They are themselves capitalists, and on no small scale. Like feudal lords they command vast areas of ten thousand acres and more. They have great sums invested in equipment and machinery —whole batteries of plows, seed drills, harvesters. They are employers of labor with scores, hundreds of men in their pay. Magnus Derrick has numerous tenants whom he turns off at his convenience. Annixter is a harsh and arbitrary master, as seen in his treatment of Delaney. He feels the agricultural employer's antipathy to the city laborer, the union man. Pausing to inspect the progress of the work on his magnificent new barn, he asks a foreman when the structure will be completed; "a precious long time you've been at it," he declares. The foreman pleads interruption on account of rain. "Oh, rot the rain!" exclaims Annixter impatiently. "*I* work in the rain. You and your unions make me sick" (p. 172).

A chance remark reveals to Presley in a flash the spirit of the gambler and individualist in Magnus Derrick. The ranchers are expecting a decision from the state railroad commission reducing freight rates (an expectation in which they are of course disappointed, since the railroad by its control of state politics virtually owns the commission). "And suppose," says Lyman Derrick, "the next commission is a railroad board, and reverses all our figures?" His father replies: "By then it will be too late. We will, all of us, have made our fortunes by then." It is the spirit of the seeker after sudden wealth, the spirit which has governed the whole economic development of the nation, which has ridden roughshod over all sense of social obligation either to the present or the future . . . .

The real struggle is between two types of economy: the one the agricultural, old and ready to pass from the scene; the other, the industrial, new and destined to dominate the future. In the press of the conflict some of the little people are crushed, people like Dyke (one time locomotive engineer on the railroad, who tries farming on his own account) and his mother and child, or like Hooven (Magnus' German tenant) and his wife and daughters. With the great wheat growers it is not a question of making a living; it is a question of running a large-scale business for profit. In other circumstances Magnus might have been Shelgrim, head of a vast railroad system, in which position he might have found himself applying the principle announced by S. Behrman to Dyke: Dyke has just learned that he has been ruined by a rise in freight charges. Promised a rate of two cents on his hops, he is confronted without warning by one of five cents; but he has already contracted to sell his crop at a certain price. Bitterly he demands to know, "What's your rule? What are you guided by?" S. Behrman, suddenly red with anger, "emphasized each word of his reply with a tap of one forefinger on the counter before him: 'All—the—traffic—will—bear' " (pp. 349-50).

The novel raises a question respecting the means to be employed in the war against social injustice. Is it legitimate to use the weapons of the enemy, to fight fire with fire? Is fraud justifiable? Is violence allowable? In the opinion of Granville Hicks, Norris leaves unsolved the problems of the use of fraud and of the use of violence. Let us examine the facts.

In the early stage of their contest with the railroad Osterman frankly proposes that the ranchers (or a secret committee of them composed of the leading figures, Annixter, the Derricks, Broderson) by means of bribery seat their own men on the commission. The corporation has checkmated them at every turn. To Osterman's mind all legitimate means have been exhausted. He realizes that the ranchers, if they adopt his scheme, run the risk of seeing their commissioners bought over by the railroad at a higher price or of seeing the hoped-for rate reductions nullified by the subservient courts. But there is no other recourse; they, too, must bribe. Magnus at first repels the idea with stern indignation. But he is placed in a painful dilemma. If the plan succeeds without him, will he refuse to participate in the benefits? Gradually, reluctantly, against every instinct and the fearful pleadings of his wife, he yields; he listens to the specious words of Annixter (p. 184): "But, Governor, standards have changed since your time; everybody plays the game now as we are playing it—the most honourable men. You can't play it any other way, and, pshaw! if the right wins in the end, that's the main thing." In the dramatic scene which concludes the chapter on the barn dance (and at the same time the first book of the novel) Magnus accepts the leadership of the defensive league spontaneously formed by the ranchers under the spur of the news, at that moment received, of the railroad's latest, most dangerous move. In doing so he also tacitly commits himself to the fraudulent tactics of the secret committee. It is a grievous mistake; a fatal error by which the cause of the ranchers suffers in the end; and for Magnus himself it is the source of his personal tragedy, a greater calamity than his material ruin, greater than the death of his son Harran.

Osterman's plan succeeds up to a point. The wheat-growers elect their men to the commission. By a crushing irony, as it proves, one of these men is Lyman Derrick, elder of Magnus' two sons, a lawyer with political ambitions, suave, deceitful, thoroughly corrupt, a born intriguer. "He belonged to the new school, wherein objects were attained not by orations before senates and assemblies, but by sessions of committees, caucuses, compromises and expedients" (p. 75). The railroad buys him with ease, and the ranchers are once more betrayed, their own dishonesty rebounding upon them. The corporation has been perfectly informed throughout of every move of its opponents. After the killing of Osterman, Annixter, and the others in the battle with the deputies, a great crowd of excited farmers and townsmen gathers in the Bonneville opera house. S. Behrman and the other local henchmen of the railroad deem this the strategic moment; and, as Magnus begins to address the meeting, by a preconcerted arrangement they cause to be thrown among the audience copies of the corporation-subsidized newspaper containing a full account of Derrick's part in the fraudulent election. Magnus stands before his friends and

all those who have trusted him a disgraced and broken man. Thus
the ranchers are outwitted at every turn, public sympathy is
alienated from them, their league breaks up, and their cause is
hopelessly lost.

Norris, writes Granville Hicks, "wavers between the view that
his [Magnus'] surrender is ignoble and the view that it is inevitable."[16] This appears to be true, for Magnus is said to be "hopelessly caught in the mesh . . . . caught in the current of events,
and hurried along he know not where," and again it is said that he
refuses to heed the voice of his better nature. Presley, however,
does not blame Magnus, but regards the moral catastrophe that
overtakes him as one more crime to be charged against the railroad.[17] Mr. Hicks complains that Magnus' ethical dilemma is unsolved. But a dilemma is by definition a situation in which either
course of action presented will lead to a bad result. It is difficult
to see what else Norris could have done. Who can deny that in the
world of actuality wrong often seems, as it seemed to Magnus
(pp. 291-92), "indissolubly knitted into the texture of Right,"
no matter how neatly these qualities are isolated in the categories
of the moralist. Norris' only error was in blaming Magnus; if he
must blame anybody he would have done better to blame Shelgrim,
who was faced with no such moral dilemma.

As regards the use of violence, none of the characters is put in
quite the hard position of Magnus with respect to the use of fraud.
The act of the ranchers in defending themselves against the
deputies will hardly be condemned. With Presley it is a little different. Filled with grief and rage by the killing of his friends, to which
he has been a witness, he spends the whole of the following night
pacing his room, or filling the pages of his journal with passionate
rushing words: "Oh, come now and try your theories upon us
. . . . Oh, talk to *us* now of the 'rights of Capital,' . . . ." And he
throws himself across his bed "vowing with inarticulate cries that
neither S. Behrman nor Shelgrim should ever live to consummate
their triumph" (pp. 538, 540). On the succeeding day, at the
indignation meeting in the Bonneville opera house, carried out of
himself, he leaps on the stage and pours out a flood of incendiary
eloquence, filled with references to the untimely fate of rulers and
painting a lurid picture of revolt (p. 552):

---

[16]Granville Hicks, *The Great Tradition* (New York, 1933), p. 173. Quoted by
permission of The Macmillan Company, publishers.
[17]*The Octopus*, pp. 291-92, 187-88, 569, 650.

> Liberty is *not* a crowned goddess, beautiful, in spotless garments,
> .... Liberty is the Man In the Street, a terrible figure, ...
> fouled with the mud and ordure of the gutter, bloody, rampant,
> brutal, yelling curses, in one hand a smoking rifle, in the other,
> a blazing torch.

There is tremendous applause, but the audience finds the speech too literary, and postpones the revolution to some indefinite date in the future.

Presley, however, is ready for some desperate act. On the previous afternoon, rushing out of the room where Harran Derrick had just died from a bullet through the lungs, he had encountered Caraher, the anarchist saloonkeeper, in the crowd gathered round the scene of the battle with the deputies. Grasping the publican by the hand he had said (p. 535): "I've been wrong all the time. The League is wrong. All the world is wrong. You are the only one of us who is right. I'm with you from now on. *By God, I too, I'm a Red!*"

Caraher's wife has been accidentally killed by Pinkertons in an encounter between these mercenaries and striking employees of the railroad. As a result he is filled with hatred for the corporation and frankly advocates violence in dealing with it. "Ah, yes," he tells Dykes when the latter has been beggared by the road, "it's all very well for your middle class to preach moderation.... That talk is just what the Trust wants to hear. It ain't frightened of that. There's one thing only it does listen to, one thing it is frightened of—the people with dynamite in their hands,—six inches of plugged gaspipe. *That* talks" (p. 357).

Inflamed by Caraher's words and maddened by the wrongs he has seen committed, Presley, on leaving the opera house, takes a bomb of the saloonkeeper's manufacture and hurls it through S. Behrman's dining-room window, just as that worthy is sitting down to his evening meal. But S. Behrman appears to be beyond the reach of human vengeance, for he emerges from the wreck of the room unscathed. He is reserved for poetic justice in more ingenious and picturesque form. But when Presley's blood has cooled he is filled with horror and remorse for what he has done, and trembles to think by what a narrow margin he has escaped the commission of murder. Later he reflects (p. 620) that Caraher is "a bad man, a plague spot in the world of the ranchers, poisoning the farmers' bodies with alcohol and their minds with discontent."

By thus repudiating violence, as he repudiates the dishonest means to which the ranchers resort, Norris provides, in fact, an answer to the question of their use. But from his assumed position of detachment it was not his business to "solve" the problem — either to sanction or to repudiate. The only way in which he could have avoided involvement was to stand unmoved on the neutral ground of his naturalism; but this, from time to time, he abandons in order to take part in the contest. In Presley's interview with Shelgrim we shall see if the author is consistent in his partisanship.

Shelgrim is president of the Pacific & Southwestern, a sinister figure who is seen only on this one occasion, but whose influence is felt in the remotest corners of his vast empire. When he pulls the strings his puppets—S. Behrman, Genslinger the editor of the Bonneville *Mercury*, Ruggles the land agent of the road in the San Joaquin, the railroad commission, judges on the bench—all move to do his will. Presley is prepared to find a monster. He finds a man of about seventy, of massive frame and equally massive composure, and a little shabby as to dress. While the poet waits to receive the attention of the great man, he overhears a conversation between him and his assistant manager concerning an employee of the road, a bookkeeper, a man competent at his task when sober, but given to periods of drunkenness. The assistant manager reminds his chief that the man in question has been repeatedly given another chance; but his latest offense is more outrageous than ever, and the assistant urges his dismissal. After a long silence during which he appears to be lost in the contemplation of matters remote from the present business, Shelgrim speaks (p. 573):

> "Tentell has a family, wife and three children. . . . . How much do we pay him?"
> "One hundred and thirty."
> "Let's double that, or say two hundred and fifty. Let's see how that will do."
> "Why—of course—if you say so, but really, Mr. Shelgrim—"
> "Well, we'll try that, anyhow."

He then turns to his visitor (whose name he recognizes at once as that of the author of "The Toilers") and delivers him a lecture, first on artistic expression and then on economics. He has read Presley's poem and he has seen the famous French painting which inspired it; "of the two, I like the picture better," he says. "You might just as well have kept quiet. There's only on best way to say anything. And what has made the picture of 'The Toilers' great is that the artist said in it the *best* that could be said on the subject." Presley is astounded. All his preconceived ideas begin to scatter. Instead of "a terrible man of blood and iron" he finds "a sentimentalist and an art critic." "He began to see that here was the man not only great, but large; many-sided, of vast sympathies, ..." When Shelgrim learns that Presley is recently from the Derrick ranch, Los Muertos, in Tulare County, he looks him fixedly in the eye and says: "I suppose you believe I am a grand old rascal." The poet stammers, and the industrial Titan proceeds to enlighten him on the economics of railroading and wheat-growing (p. 576):

> . . . . "*Railroads build themselves.* Where there is a demand sooner or later there will be a supply. Mr. Derrick, does he grow his wheat? The Wheat grows itself. What does he count for? Does he supply the force? What do I count for? Do I build the Railroad? . . . . The Wheat is one force, the Railroad, another, and there is the law that governs them—supply and demand . . . . Blame conditions, not men."
>
> "But—but," faltered Presley, "you are the head, you control the road."
>
> "You are a very young man. Control the road! Can I stop it? I can go into bankruptcy if you like. But otherwise if I run my road, as a business proposition, I can do nothing . . . . Can your Mr. Derrick stop the Wheat growing? He can burn his crops, or he can give it away, or sell it for a cent a bushel . . . . but otherwise his Wheat must grow. Can anyone stop the Wheat? Well, then no more can I stop the Road."

Presley allows himself to be completely fogged by these resounding sophistries, which in his ear "rang with the clear reverberation of truth" but which ought not to have deceived a schoolboy. He permits himself to be confused by the generosity of Shelgrim toward the drunken bookkeeper, thus tumbling into the "good man" fallacy which Macaulay so brilliantly exploded in connection with the domestic virtues of Charles I.

But Shelgrim's generosity is merely capricious. It falls where the occasion for it comes immediately under his eye. Dyke has been a faithful servant of the road; he has even refused to strike against it, continuing to run his train at some danger to his life. But he is only one of thousands whom Shelgrim has never seen, and when it is deemed expedient to cut wages he suffers along with all other employees; when he protests he is let go without any show of reluctance.

Shelgrim cannot hide so easily behind his impersonal forces. When he bids Presley "blame conditions, not men," he offers us an opponent very slippery in the grasp. Conditions, like principles, like ideals, manifest themselves only through men. Too easily, "bad" conditions become an abstraction like sin. One is tempted to believe here that Ambrose Bierce was right when he wrote:

> Sin is not at all dangerous to society; what does all the mischief is the sinner. . . . I would no more attack [crime] than I would attack an isosceles triangle . . . . My chosen enemy must be something that has a skin for my switch . . . . I have no quarrel with abstractions; so far as I know they are all good citizens.[18]

The naturalists laid out a very severe course when by committing themselves to determinism and consequent moral aloofness they attempted to deny themselves the luxury of blaming wrongdoers. Not to blame is too much for human nature; not to believe that effects must follow their causes is too much for human reason. We must continue to face the hard saying of Scripture: "It must needs be that offences come, but woe unto him by whom the offence cometh." It need not surprise that Norris should blame some of his characters, but only that he should be so maladroit as to blame the wrong ones.

If we are to accept Shelgrim's interpretation of events, the only alternative to bribery, corruption, extortion, and wrecked lives is the bankruptcy of the railroad, a patent absurdity. There is no question of bankruptcy. Harran Derrick knows better. He knows that the road was constructed for fifty-four thousand dollars a mile, but that freight rates and dividends to stockholders are based on a cost of eighty-seven thousand, and on a gross overvaluation of the whole vast property—a trick as common among corporations as brass knuckles among ruffians. He knows that the fine-sounding phrase "a fair return on our investment," which rolls so righteously off the tongue of S. Behrman, conceals all the devious and intricate deceptions of corporation finance.

Norris wants us to believe that the cause of the ranchers is just,

---

[18]*The Shadow on the Dial and Other Essays* (San Francisco: A. M. Robertson, 1909), pp. 123-24.

wants us to sympathize with them. He puts himself, however, in the position of holding them to account for their lapses from virtue in their struggle with the railroad (though they have been hounded and harried beyond endurance) but at the same time of allowing Shelgrim to take refuge behind the laws of supply and demand, behind "conditions," impersonal forces. When Presley descended to the street after his interview with the great industrialist, his whole scheme of values in disarray, Norris walked arm in arm with him and shared his bewilderment. It is to be suspected that he described his own state when he wrote that Presley, after devouring works on sociology and economics, "emerged from the affair, his mind a confused jumble of conflicting notions, ... raging against injustice and oppression, and with not one sane suggestion as to remedy or redress."

But if, like his ineffectual reformer, he is a bit dazzled by the philosophic splendor of the law of supply and demand, he feels nevertheless a genuine and poignant concern for the poor and outcast. The sore contradiction of poverty in the midst of wealth weighs on his mind, and when he speaks of it he cannot suppress a note of scorn and reproof for the complacently well-fed, the secure, and the smug. So intent is he on driving home this contrast between want and luxury that he prolongs his narrative beyond the dramatic close of the main action in order to record the fate of Mrs. Hooven. After the death of Hooven with the others in the fight at the irrigation ditch, his wife goes to San Francisco in search of work. Her small funds are soon gone and she and the child Hilda are put out of their lodgings into the street. She has not a penny in the world, nor a friend except Presley, who knows not where to seek her. She feels all a countrywoman's bewilderment and terror in the midst of the strangeness and indifference of a great city, where the faces in endless procession reflect, as it seems to her, "every emotion but pity." As she stands helpless on the sidewalk a policeman, for this crime against public order, commands her to move on and threatens her with arrest. Now begins the aimless, hopeless march that leads to her miserable death. . . .

Meantime Presley, through his aunt, Mrs. Cedarquist, wife of the manufacturer, has been asked to dine at the home of Gerard, one of the vice-presidents of the Pacific & Southwestern, in ignorance, be it said, of the identity of his host till he has reached the door. Again Norris' millionaires are of the first generation, a little raw as yet, still marked by the crudities of the newly rich, essentially vulgar. The women, who sprinkle their conversation with French, coo over Presley. "I have read your poem, of course, ... What a sermon you read us, you dreadful young man," his hostess chides gayly. "I felt that I ought at once to 'sell all that I have and give to the poor,'" she assures him, though she has been successful in resisting this impulse. The magnificent drawing room is minutely described, with its Renaissance cabinets of ebony inlaid with ivory and silver and its brass andirons six feet high for the huge fireplace. Then Presley sits down to a dinner that is a gastronomic master-piece—course after course: "raw Blue Point oysters, served upon little pyramids of shaved ice," ortolan patties, "*grenadins* of bass and small salmon, the latter stuffed, and cooked in white wine and mushroom liquor," "Londonderry pheasants, escallops of duck, and *rissolettes à la pompadour*," stuffed artichokes. The asparagus, the guests are informed, comes from a particular ranch in the southern part of the state; it is ordered by wire and put on a special train which makes a special stop to take it aboard. "Extrav-agant, isn't it," the hostess deprecates, "but I simply cannot eat asparagus that has been cut more than a day." Several of the wines are from Gerard's private vineyards in southern France. As Presley sips his Xeres 1815 and looks about at his sumptuous surroundings and the exquisite women seated at the board, he reflects: "It was Wealth, in all its outward and visible forms, the signs of an opu-lence so great that it need never be husbanded. . . . For this, then, the farmers paid." He is not entirely satisfied with Shelgrim's explanation, and a sequence of cause and effect seems plain to him which Shelgrim would refuse to accept: "The Railroad might in-deed be a force only, which no man could control and for which no man was responsible, but his friends had been killed . . . because the farmers of the valley were poor, these men were rich." Then a strange fancy enters his mind, a grotesque transformation of the present banquet (p. 608):

> It was a half-ludicrous, half-horrible "dog-eat-dog," an unspeakable cannibalism. Harran, Annixter, and Hooven were being devoured there under his eyes. These dainty women, ... with their small fingers and slender necks, suddenly were transfigured in his tor-tured mind into harpies tearing human flesh.

From time to time Norris interrupts the progress of the feast to follow the ever feebler footsteps of Mrs. Hooven. Four nights she and the child have spent on park benches, shivering with cold, wetted with fog, and surrounded by drunken derelicts. Every day she has begged in the streets, collecting a few dimes and nickels to buy bread and milk for little Hilda. It was by accident that she fell into this last humiliation. A passer-by whom she stopped to ask a direction had misunderstood her and put a quarter in her hand. For three days she herself has eaten nothing but a few apples and crust of bread rescued from the street. By the night of Mrs. Gerard's dinner she is far gone, wracked by pains and cramps in the stomach, faint and dizzy, hardly able to bear the weight of the sleeping child in her arms. At about the moment when the diners are engaged on their stuffed salmon cooked in white wine and mushroom liquor, or perhaps their Londonderry pheasants, Mrs. Hooven finds on the sidewalk the peeling of a banana:

> "Hilda," she cried, "wake oop, leedle girl. See, loog den, dere's somedings to eat. Look den, hey? Dat's goot, ain't it? Zum bunaner."
> But it could not be eaten. Decayed, dirty, all but rotting, the stomach turned from the refuse, nauseated.

The dessert, "a wonderful preparation of alternate layers of biscuit glacés, ice cream, and candied chestnuts," arrived at the instant when Mrs. Hooven lay down to die in a vacant lot atop a wind-swept, fog-drenched hill in a thinly peopled part of the city. A pleasant coma stole over her, and gradually she ceased to respond to the frightened pleadings of the child. She was dead. "The gaunt, lean body, with its bony face and sunken eye-sockets, lay back, prone upon the ground, the feet upturned and showing the ragged, worn soles of the shoes, the forehead and gray hair beaded with fog . . ."

The extended account of Mrs. Hooven's wretched end, contrasted with riches which insult by their very existence, has been called melodramatic. Forming, as it does, a postscript to the principal narrative, it may be regarded as a structural defect. Criticism, however, is forever disconcerted by the fact that a good novel has never been seriously injured by structural defects, any more than a bad one is saved by structural perfection. Critics have raised superior eyebrows at the pathos of the episode. Its pathos is nevertheless sounder than that of a score of scenes in Dickens, or even in some of his less tearful contemporaries. The details are harder, sharper; the tone (except for the *via dolorosa* passage) less emotional.

Walter Fuller Taylor

From *The Economic Novel in America*

The Octopus, outgrowth as it is of Norris's admiration for the "big" novel, really puts on record in vigorous narrative an entire regional society; economic conflict is only the dominant one among its several themes. The principal story is, of course, that of the struggle between the ranchers and the railroad for the possession of the fertile wheat lands of the San Joaquin valley. It is in itself a multiple story, including as its main thread of interest the tragedy of the leader of the ranchers, Magnus Derrick, and as minor threads the bearing of the railroad-rancher struggle on the lives of a dozen sharply conceived though technically subordinate characters. Associated with this major story, tied in with it by a hundred interlinking threads, are at least three fully developed minor plots: the contest between the railroad and the discharged engineer, Dyke; the love story of Hilma Tree and the rancher Annixter; and the idyl of Vanamee and the two Angéles. And besides all these, even, the immense network of narrative encloses and bears along a num-

Reprinted from *The Economic Novel in America* (Chapel Hill: The University of North Carolina Press, 1942), 282-306, by permission of the University of North Carolina Press.

ber of subsidiary episodes, like the sketches of Father Sarria and of the fate of the Hooven family, which are associated with some one of the several plots, though not essential to it.

The characters of *The Octopus*, like its immensely complex narrative, cover virtually the entire range of an entire social order. . . .

And as these numerous and varied characters comprise virtually an entire Folk, so the various scenes and episodes of *The Octopus* comprise what might be called—no doubt inexactly—the Folk-experience of their region, which was in considerable measure the folk-experience of late-nineteenth-century America. Superficially, this typical quality of the book appears in Norris's portrayal of Western usages and folkways and customs: the rabbit drive, the gigantic plowing at Los Muertos, the dance at Annixter's barn. More fundamentally, it appears in his truly remarkable grasp of the most significant and central *economic* experiences of his generation. Whether deliberately so intended or not, the struggle between the ranchers and the railway monopoly typifies the most far-reaching and important class conflict of that age in America, the conflict between the middle classes and the plutocracy; and the main issue between ranchers and railroad—the disposal of the public lands[38]—has been from the very beginnings of America one of those half dozen absolutely primary factors that have shaped the entire course of our economic history. Equally central in the experience of the Gilded Age is the struggle of the two opposed groups for political control, together with the resulting corruption of all branches of government by the influence of victorious Big Business.[39] And besides these more significant and typical economic problems, *The Octopus* treats still others: problems of speculative business, such as stock-watering; problems of labor, such as unemployment, labor insecurity, and the blacklist; problems of railway control, such as those growing out of obstructive shipping regulations and the practice of charging all the traffic will bear.[40] In its industrial bearings alone, it appears, *The Octopus* comes very near summing up the American experience of economics from the Civil War to 1900; and in the largeness and the multiplicity of its total materials—story, characters, subject-matter, ideas—it can be com-

---

[38]For this phase of the story, see especially Vol I. pp. 264 ff.

[39]For examples of the treatment of this subject in *The Octopus,* see I: 102-13, II: 6, 154 ff., *et al.*

[40]See, for examples, *The Octopus,* I: 15, 63-6.

pared only with those Hugoesque, Tolstoyesque leviathans of fiction that Norris was emulating.

The Octopus is as admirably organized as it is big. The structural
mechanics of the book—in exposition, preparation, interweaving
of plots, and handling of climaxes—are both sound and ingenious
enough to challege comparison with those of that masterpiece of
structure, *Tom Jones;* and the net effect is just that deliberate
beginning, that steady acceleration of movement, and that final
onrush of overwhelming power which in other novels Norris had
so much admired. Moreover, once the book gets under way, it is,
as Norris intended, a thrilling, hair-lifting story, a story almost too
crowded with adventurous incident. Here, as in his earlier stories,
Norris discovers excitement chiefly in the resurgence into civilized
life of primitive passions and the primitive struggle for survival;
he all but over-insists on the presentation of man as a fighting
animal. The fury of the ranchers, at the meeting where they learn
of the railroad's ruinous prices on land, becomes to him "the
hideous squealing of the tormented brute, its back to the wall,
defending its lair"; the excitement of the posse trailing the fugi-
tive Dyke is that of "the trackers exulting on the trail of the
pursued." In Norris's earlier writing, such episodes had frequently
failed to "come off"; in *The Octopus,* supported by the whole
texture of story and by the force of a maturer imagination, they
become natural, credible, and powerful.

. . . Now it is in just this matter of philosophical consistency
that Norris, in *The Octopus,* falls short. For, on the one hand, he
interprets his story at times by a philosophy of free will, according
to which life is a moral experience, and man a being of importance;
and, on the other hand, he interprets his story at other times by
an optimistic determinism, according to which life is an amoral
experience, and the individual man of no importance in comparison
with the total life-scheme. It is the moral viewpoint which controls
the story of Annixter's development in character under the influence of Hilma Tree,[45] which gives tragic meaning to the story of
Magnus Derrick's decline,[46] and which motivates throughout most
of the story Presley's fierce indignation against the railroad.[47] It is
the amoral, deterministic viewpoint which evokes Shelgrim's advice
to Presley, "Blame conditions, not men"; which finds voice in

---

[45]*The Octopus,* pp. 118, 148.
[46]Ibid., II: 113. Observe also the moral implications of such a phrase as "the
anguish of compromise with conscience" (II, 171).
[47]For example, *ibid.,* II, 23.

Vanamee's optimistic fatalism, and which leaves with Presley, at last, the consolation of faith in the cosmic Force that, although indifferent to the individual, works irresistibly toward the total good.[48] But the reader, who has received so much of the story through the medium of Presley's earlier, moral point of view, is nowhere prepared for this sudden change of front, so that the large optimism of the concluding pages, instead of serving its apparent purpose of closing the terrible story upon a level of serene reconciliation, has rather the disconcerting effect of a verdict given against the evidence. The reader feels (to speak impressionistically) that he has been witnessing a flurry of hectic action without meaning, a spectacle sufficiently dramatic and thrilling, but of doubtful significance, or none at all. And therefore *The Octopus*, fine achievement that it is, is still not so fine as it might well have been could Norris have equalled in orderly thinking his excellence in keen perception and dramatic force.[49]

---

[48]*Ibid.*, II, 285, 344-5, 359-61, respectively.

[49]See, for a detailed and thoughtful study of the problem of Norris's philosophical inconsistency, Charles Child Walcutt, *Naturalism in the American Novel*. A doctoral dissertation of the University of Michigan (Ann Arbor, 1937), pp. 247-351. For a contrary opinion—namely, that Norris was philosophically consistent—see H. Willard Reninger, "Norris explains *The Octopus:* a Correlation of His Theory and Practice," *American Literature*, XII: 218-27 (May, 1940); and for a rejoinder, pointing out certain errors in Reninger's treatment, Charles Child Walcutt, "Frank Norris on Realism and Naturalism," *American Literature*, XIII: 61-3 (March, 1941).

George Wilbur Meyer

A New Interpretation of
The Octopus

Since its publication in 1901, Frank Norris' *The Octopus* has
been variously described by many scholars and critics, most of
whom agree that the book, despite its numerous virtues, cannot
be regarded as a novel of the first rank. In 1915, Fred Lewis Pattee
asserted that *The Octopus* and its sequel, *The Pit*, were "not
literature," that they tended "no whither" and came to "no ter-
minus of conclusion."[2] In 1926, Thomas Beer, with a definition of
"literature" different from that of Professor Pattee, objected to
The Octopus on the ground that Norris made "Jehovah thunder
at the close" and by so doing reduced an otherwise admirable
work to a heap of moralistic rubbish.[3] In 1930, Vernon Louis
Parrington gave academic weight to Beer's argument by remarking
that at the end of *The Octopus* Norris "abandons the amoral attitude .... [and] takes refuge in a moral order."[4]

Reprinted from *College English,* IV (March 1943), 351-359, with the permission of the National Council of Teachers of English and George Wilbur
Meyer.
[2]*A History of American Literature since 1870* (New York, 1915), p. 400.
[3]*The Mauve Decade* (Garden City, N.Y., 1936), p. 99.
[4]*Main Currents in American Thought* (New York, 1930), III, 333.

Then, in the early nineteen-thirties, *The Octopus* was discovered by critics who, heavy with the theories of Karl Marx, were more eager to find evidence of bourgeois criminality and proletarian virtue in American fiction than they were accurate in interpreting the novels which seemed to serve their purpose best. In 1932 and 1933, respectively, John Chamberlain and Granville Hicks observed that *The Octopus*, despite the economic significance of its subject, missed greatness because of its confused, moralistic, and thoroughly "specious" ending.[5] This seems to have been their way of saying that the book did not conform in every detail to the regulation formula of the proletarian novel. More recently, Walter Fuller Taylor, repeating these basic charges, accuses Norris of vacillating irresponsibly between a philosophy of free will and one of optimistic determinism; according to him, the ending of *The Octopus* is simply "a verdict given against the evidence."[6]

These critics contend, in brief, that *The Octopus*—Norris' masterpiece and a landmark in the history of American naturalism—contains disparate elements which Norris could not fuse into a satisfactory artistic whole. These supposedly disparate elements are a philosophy of determinism, a tragic action set in a vicious society, and an optimistic conclusion which suggests that the good will triumph in the end. This study presents an interpretation of *The Octopus* that reconciles these aparently incompatible aspects of the novel. It suggests, moreover, that previous critics of Norris have misunderstood one of the fundamental problems of the naturalistic philosophy—the distinction between determinism and fatalism—and have mistaken at least two of Norris' characters for Norris himself.

. . . In *The Octopus*, the subject of which is the struggle between the California farmers and the Pacific and Southwestern Railroad for control of a crop of wheat, Norris' particular purposes seem to have been three: (1) to show by means of the symbol of the wheat the immutability of the natural order; (2) to demonstrate that the American socioeconomic system of the late nineteenth century was maladjusted to nature and was, consequently, the cause of unnecessary social evil; and (3) to suggest to his readers the need for reforming the American system along the naturalistic lines briefly sketched for them in the novel.

---

[5]John Chamberlain, *Farewell to Reform* (New York, 1932), pp. 105-10; Granville Hicks, *The Great Tradition* (New York, 1933), pp. 171-73.
[6]*The Economic Novel in America* (Chapel Hill, N.C., 1942), p. 299.

The philosophic first premise of *The Octopus* is the notion that the wheat will flow irresistibly from the fields where it is grown to mouths that need to be fed. Since Norris presented this idea not as a mere theory but as a fundamental law of nature, an understanding of its implications is indispensable to any sound interpretation of the novel. According to Norris, the wheat moves from the fields to regions of famine as inevitably as masses of air move from high to lower areas of barometric pressure. Obstacles in its path may retard its progress or alter its course, but the goal is invariably attained. This tendency of the wheat should not, however, be regarded as evidence that the natural order is intelligent, purposive, or benign. Ultimately, it is true, the wheat benefits those masses of the people who use it for food. But it is also true that the natural force represented by the wheat in *The Octopus* injures or destroys many individuals unlucky enough to be standing in its path. Nature thus might appear to be both benign and malevolent, depending upon the point of view. Actually she is neither. She is merely a fact, established and eternal. She can be both creative and destructive. Which she will be depends for the most part upon man's ability first to understand and then to adjust himself to her changeless laws.

Norris appears to have designed the main action of *The Octopus* to illustrate his conviction that Americans wrought unnecessary evil by supporting an economic system that clashed violently with manifest facts of nature. After introducing his main characters and briefly defining the issues of the conflict in which they are engaged, Norris devotes the fourth chapter of the book to presenting his conception of the wheat and to establishing a norm for his criticism of American society.

In a passage that emphasizes the dynamic fertility of nature, Norris begins by describing the land, the unplowed fields of the San Joaquin after the first rain of early spring:

> All about between the horizons, the carpet of the land unrolled itself to infinity. But now it was no longer parched with heat, cracked and warped by a merciless sun, powdered with dust. The rain had done its work; not a clod that was not swollen with fertility, not a fissure that did not exhale the sense of fecundity. One could not take a dozen steps upon the ranches without the brusque sensation that underfoot the land was alive; roused at last from its sleep, palpitating with the desire of reproduction. Deep down there in the recesses of the soil, the great heart throbbed once more, thrilling with passion, vibrating with desire, offering itself to the caress

of the plow, insistent, eager, imperious. Dimly one felt the deep-seated trouble of the earth, the uneasy agitation of its members, the hidden tumult of its womb, demanding to be made fruitful, to reproduce, to disengage the eternal renascent germ of Life that stirred and struggled in its loins.[8]

Then, in the overwrought but important conclusion to his account of the plowing, Norris expresses his idea of the fundamental relationship of man to nature:

It was the long stroking caress, vigorous, male, powerful, for which the Earth seemed panting. The heroic embrace of a multitude of iron hands, gripping deep into the brown, warm flesh of the land that quivered responsive and passionate under this rude advance, so robust as to be almost an assault, so violent as to be veritably brutal. There, under the sun and under the speckless sheen of the sky, the wooing of the Titan began, the vast primal passion, the two world-forces, the elemental Male and Female, locked in a colossal embrace, at grapples in the throes of an infinite desire, at once terrible and divine, knowing no law, untamed, savage, natural, sublime.[9]

Finally, through the character Vanamee, Norris comments explicitly upon the significance of the life led by the hardy ranchers in the vital season when the land is ready to replenish the earth with a crop of wheat:

Vanamee, simple, uncomplicated, living so close to nature and the rudimentary life, understood its significance. . . . . Work, food, and sleep, all life reduced to its bare essentials, uncomplex, honest, healthy. They were strong, these men, with the strength of the soil they worked, in touch with the essential things, back again to the starting point of civilization, coarse, vital, real, and sane.[10]

These passages reveal a group of men engaged co-operatively with nature in the act of reproduction. Knowing by experience, and perhaps by instinct, when it is time to plow and plant the seed, the farmers perform the male function of impregnating the fertile soil. While they are thus engaged, they lead unsophisticated lives; they exist, like the legendary noble savage of the eighteenth cen-

[8]*The Octopus* (New York, 1901), p. 95.
[9]*Ibid.*, p. 98.
[10]*Ibid.*, p. 99.

tury, in a happy state of nature. Such an existence represents
Norris' idea of a rational adjustment of men to their environment.
As long as men live such a life, they are "honest healthy. . . . strong
. . . . in touch with the essential things, back again to the starting
point of civilization, coarse, vital, real, and sane." As long as men
maintain this harmonious relationship with the natural order, their
actions are good and useful, for, by exploiting successfully her
potentialities as an agency of humane and social purpose, they give
to nature the appearance of intelligent benignity.

But the farmers of *The Octopus* live double lives. To their mis-
fortune, they do not long remain at "the starting point of civilization." Once they have played their part in the titanic love affair,
they return to the chaotic world of late-nineteenth-century America
—to the competitive world of the railway trust and the bulls and
bears, and to that overwhelming desire for private profit which
dwarfs all other values in their society. They do not remain elemental aspects of the male force in nature; instead, they become
selfish individualists, social and economic anarchists out to make
a fortune at any cost. In so far as they pursue this selfish purpose,
they are at odds with nature and their actions are evil and socially
injurious. To an account of this perverse portion of their behavior
and its tragic social consequences Frank Norris devotes the bulk
of his novel.

One cause of the confusion in previous comment upon *The
Octopus* seems to have been a general misunderstanding of Norris'
estimate of the California farmers. This is especially true of the
remarks of those critics whose belligerent sympathy for the defeated in any conflict resembling a class struggle leads them to
regard the ranchers as a group of persecuted innocents. If Norris'
descriptions of them are valid evidence, however, it is clear that
Magnus Derrick and his confederates were not created to represent
the old frontier individualism before that individualism was strangled in the iron grip of big business.[11] Despite their superficial
resemblance to an earlier type, these late-nineteenth-century farmers are not pathetic relics of Jeffersonian agrarianism forced to live
in a society dedicated to Mammon and the principles of Alexander
Hamilton.[12] Norris' wheat-growers have little in common with the
toil-worn countrymen of the Middle Border whom we encounter

---

[11]See V. F. Calverton, *The Liberation of American Literature* (New York,
1932), pp. 350 and 352.
[12]Chamberlain, *op. cit.* p. 109.

in the works of Hamlin Garland. They are even less like the itin-
erant ranch-hands of Steinbeck's *Of Mice and Men* or those desperate creatures of *The Grapes of Wrath,* who, torn by the superior
economic dislocations of the twentieth century, struggle to work
for a few cents an hour that they may enjoy an evenings meal.
Compared to the people of Garland and Steinbeck, Norris' characters are lords of creation: the former lack the necessities of
existence; the ranchers of *The Octopus* think in terms of large
fortunes. The Joads are like children beaten for reasons of which
they are ignorant; Magnus Derrick and his fellow-conspirators are
sufficiently endowed with cash and information to plan and launch
a counterattack against the railroad trust. It is a serious mistake
to believe that Norris regarded his farmers as mere symbols of an
abused proletariat. The truth is that he saw them as reckless
would-be profiteers, as speculators so unfortunate as to be less
powerful and ingenious than their competitors in a ruinous struggle
for economic power.

Norris insists that the ranchers of the San Joaquin were ruthless
exploiters of the soil who plotted to manipulate freight rates with
the single purpose of acquiring fortunes from one gigantic crop of
wheat. His emphasis upon this fact is clearly seen in his preliminary
sketch of the character of Magnus Derrick, the noblest rancher of
them all, according to conventional ethical standards:

> He was always ready to take chances, to hazard everything on
> the hopes of colossal returns. In the mining days at Placerville
> there was no more redoubtable poker player in the county. He had
> been as lucky in his mines as in his gambling, sinking shafts and
> tunneling in violation of expert theory and finding "pay" in every
> case. Without knowing it, he allowed himself to work his ranch
> much as if he was still working his mine. The old-time spirit of
> '49, haphazard, unscientific, persisted in his mind. Everything was
> a gamble—who took the greatest chances was most apt to be the
> greatest winner. The idea of manuring Los Muertos, of husbanding
> his great resources, he would have scouted as niggardly, Hebraic,
> ungenerous.[13]

Further on, Norris affirms that these salient features of Magnus'
character—his gambling instinct, his willingness to exploit his land
to the utmost, his selfishness—were not peculiar to Magnus but

---

[13]*The Octopus,* p. 51.

were typical of the ranchers as a group. Magnus was sure that it would be necessary to "fix" only one rate commission. He did not worry lest a later commission undo the work of the first: "By then," he says, "it will be too late. We will, all of us, have made our fortunes by then."

> That was it precisely [Norris explains]. "After us the deluge."
> . . . . It was in this frame of mind that Magnus and the multitude of other ranchers of whom he was a type farmed their ranches. They had no love for their land. They were not attached to the soil.
> . . . . To get all there was out of the land, to squeeze it dry, to exhaust it, seemed their policy. When, at last, the land, worn out, would refuse to yield, they would invest their money in something else; by then, they would all have made fortunes. They did not care. "After us the deluge."[14]

Probably because he tells the story of *The Octopus* from the point of view of the farmers, Norris provides no detailed appraisal of the men who work for the railroad. It is plain enough, however, that he regards them, like the farmers, as agents of both good and evil and that he conceives of the railroad itself as a part of the dynamic order of nature. Such at least appears to be the meaning of the speech made by Shelgrim, the president of the Pacific and Southwestern, when he tries to give Presley a sound explanation of the unfortunate massacre at Magnus Derrick's irrigation ditch:

> " . . . . *Railroads build themselves.* Where there is a demand sooner or later there will be a supply. Mr. Derrick, does he grow his wheat? The Wheat grows itself. What does he count for? Does he supply the force? What do I count for? Do I build the Railroad? You are dealing with forces . . . . when you speak of Wheat and the Railroads, not with men. There is the Wheat, the supply. It must be carried to feed the People. There is the demand. The Wheat is one force, the Railroad, another, and there is the law that governs them—supply and demand. Men have only little to do in the whole business. Complications may arise, conditions that bear hard on the individual—crush him maybe—*but the Wheat will be carried to feed the people* as inevitably as it will grow. If you want to fasten the blame of the affair at Los Muertos on any one person, you will make a mistake. Blame conditions, not men."[15]

---

[14]*Ibid.*, pp. 216-17.
[15]*Ibid.*, p. 147. The italics are Norris'.

According to this, as long as the railroad men work to fulfil the manifest purpose of the railroad—as long, that is, as they strive to make the railroad an efficient carrier of food to the people—they are well adjusted to their environment, and their actions are of indisputable benefit to society. But when, like the ranchers, they interfere with the growth and transportation of the wheat; when they plot and conspire, break contracts and bribe, tamper with the law of supply and demand for personal gain; then they become the authors of evil which their leader, Shelgrim, erroneously attributes to the natural order.

II

Shelgrim's conclusion that "conditions, not men" were to blame for the massacre at the irrigation ditch is fallacious, for it is obvious that the faulty "conditions" were produced by men who meddled with the wheat and the railroad—forces which in themselves are quite innocuous. One of Norris' main purposes in *The Octopus* was to criticize the unnatural society of late-nineteenth-century America. This he did by describing pointedly those conditions—actually created by men motivated by a lust for profit—for which Shelgrim fatalistically holds the natural order of things responsible. These conditions include, among others, the unjust discharge and blacklisting by employers of faithful employees; the flagrant violation of verbal contracts, the corruption by bribery of public officials and the custodians of the agencies of written communication, blackmail, starvation in the midst of plenty, the ruthless exploitation of natural resources, and a tragic waste of men, work, and material. But the outstanding and most reprehensible condition produced by men in this socioeconomic system is the appearance of senselessness that characterizes virtually all human endeavor. The chief characteristic of the society described in *The Octopus* is the abject submission of its members to the irrational force of chance.

The fact that chance governs the fate of the majority of the characters in *The Octopus* is established by the two most sensational incidents in the book. It is chance, after all—chance set free by misdirected human action—that kills the ranchers at the irrigation ditch. And it is chance that destroys S. Behrman in the hold of the "Swanhilda." Such an accident as Behrman's cannot of course be prevented by any socioeconomic system,[16] but situations like that at the irrigation ditch need not occur. At Los Muertos the opportunity to murder the farmers and the agents of the railroad was given to chance by the peculiar economic interests of the men involved. For months these men had been working at cross-purposes, distrusting, hating, and fearing one another, forgetful of the manifest facts of nature, mindful only of the first principle of late-nineteenth-century economics—"Dog eat dog and the devil take the hindmost." When at last they faced one another armed, the individuals on both sides were predisposed to fire on their competitors at the slightest provocation. Chance then intervened to provide the overwrought ranchers with what appeared to be an unmistakable sign of active belligerence in the ranks of their opponents.

The real tragedy of the irrigation ditch is that men should have given chance such a favorable opportunity to express itself. It is this tragedy—the decisive interference of chance in human affairs —that is chiefly responsible for the senselessness which Theodore Dreiser and other pessimists discover in their studies of the universe. Unlike the pessimists, who are content to describe mere appearances, Norris suggests that chance, and the disorder caused by its pervasive influence in society, may be for the most part eliminated if men will co-operate with one another and adjust themselves to nature. Until men do so co-operate and gear their socioeconomic system to the inflexible cogs of nature's vast machine, they must expect to suffer a thousand unnatural shocks that human flesh is not necessarily heir to.

III

With this understanding of the first two of Norris' three chief purposes in *The Octopus*, it is not difficult to discover his final

---

[16]John Chamberlain's suggestion that the death of Behrman represents Norris' "sudden panicky concession" to the conventions of genteel fiction (*op cit.*, pp. 108 and 109) or his attempt to moralize "in the interests of an impossible poetic justice" (*ibid.*, p. 105), does not fit all the facts of the novel. Had Norris wished to give *The Octopus* a poetically just ending, he would have destroyed Shelgrim and Lyman Derrick. Behrman is merely Shelgrim's agent and tool. Shelgrim, as president of the railroad, is the greatest source of evil in the book. Next to him in importance is Lyman Derrick, the ingrate son, who double-crosses his father and brother to further his political ambitions. Near the end of the book Presley discovers that Lyman is running for the office of governor of California. Since he has the support of the politically omnipotent Pacific and Southwestern, he is certain to be elected. Such a reward for the treacherous Lyman serves neither morality nor poetic justice.

purpose—that of persuading his readers to reform their society. Neither is it impossible now to reconcile those elements of the novel which most critics have thus far found irreconcilable: the philosophy of determinism, the description of a tragic action in an ugly society, and the optimistic doctrines, voiced by Vanamee and Presley, with which Norris chose to end his novel.

According to the philosophy of determinism, it is plain that none of the characters in *The Octopus* may be blamed for his contribution to the general socioeconomic disorder in which he exists.[17] It is true that the perverse actions of Magnus Derrick and S. Behrman give to the forces of nature—the wheat and the railroad —the false appearance of deliberate malevolence. But this is not to say that Derrick and Behrman are guilty of deliberate misbehavior. They cannot be held morally responsible for their unnatural endeavors, because their characters have been determined by environmental factors beyond their control. They participate willingly in an unnatural system of economics because they have been taught to believe that such a system is natural and inevitable. They tamper with natural forces in the hope of personal gain, not because they are essentially vicious, but because they fail to understand nature and her laws. They err through ignorance, and in their ignorance lies their innocence. Shelgrim alone among them approaches knowledge of the truth; but even he, reasoning—or rather rationalizing—from sound premises, reaches conclusions that are false.

The fact that the tragedy of *The Octopus* was determined by forces which the characters of the novel could not control, and that it was therefore inevitable, does not mean that the tragedy must inevitably be repeated. Neither does the fact that Magnus Derrick and S. Behrman must be absolved of moral responsibility for their actions mean that all men forever shall be guiltless for similar behavior. Unlike many of his critics, Frank Norris did not

---

[17]Granville Hicks contends that Norris, in his account of the downfall of Magnus Derrick, "wavers between the view that his surrender is ignoble and the view that it is inevitable" (*op. cit.*, p. 173). But Norris' interpretation of Magnus' character seems to me perfectly consistent. Norris suggests that the forces of heredity and environment, in addition to a kind of instinct to revolt against injustice, compelled Magnus to accept the position of president of the League and later to engage in corrupt practices. Once Magnus has regained his composure, the ethical scruples of the society in which he was born and bred overwhelm him and make him ashamed of his immorality (see *The Octopus*, pp. 211 and 212). But this is Magnus judging himself, not Norris passing judgment on one of his characters.

confuse determinism with fatalism.[18] He did not believe that what
had happened once must necessarily happen again. Specifically,
he did not believe that the socioeconomic confusion of the world
he lived in—the world described in *The Octopus*—was predestined
to continue throughout eternity. Norris was confident that the
people were capable of correcting old errors and of reforming a
society that was unsatisfactory. His belief that the people waited
only for information and for some external force to rouse them to
constructive action is expressed near the beginning of the second
book of *The Octopus* by Cedarquist, the shipbuilder, when he
observes that the greatest evil in American life is "the indifference
of the better people to public affairs."[19] Economic injustice and
despotism, according to Cedarquist, exist only by permission of
the people: they "have but to say 'No,' and not the strongest
tyranny, political, religious, or financial, that was ever organized,
could survive one week."[20]

Norris, like his master, Émile Zola, thought that the novel could
and should be made to educate the people in the determinism of
social evil and to stimulate in them the determination to say "No"
to all forms of injustice and despotism. In his essay "The Novel
with a 'Purpose,' " Norris insists that the novel

> may be a great force, that works together with the pulpit and the
> universities for the good of the people, fearlessly proving that
> power is abused, that the strong grind the faces of the weak, that
> an evil tree is still growing in the midst of the garden. . . . .[21]

In *The Octopus*, Norris attempted to make the novel such a force.
By emphasizing the immutability of nature, by describing the
human suffering and waste that result from laissez faire economics,
and by outlining his conception of a healthy adjustment of men
to those parts of their environment which cannot be changed,

---

[18]The confusion of determinism with fatalism seems to be responsible for the
widespread beliefs that all naturalistic writers are pessimists and that any
naturalistic novel which ends optimistically, as does *The Octopus,* must be
philosophically incoherent. For a discussion of the distinction between determinism and fatalism and for proof that the naturalistic novel, as Émile Zola
originally conceived of it, was optimistic rather than pessimistic in its
philosophical tendency, see my article, "The Original Social Purpose of the
Naturalistic Novel," *Sewanee Review,* L (October-December, 1942), 563-70.
[19]*The Octopus,* p. 221.
[20]*Ibid.*
[21]*The Responsibilities of the Novelist* (New York, 1903), p. 32.

Norris hoped to move his readers to intelligent reformatory action. Whether or not his readers were so moved, this much at least should be certain: although Magnus Derrick and S. Behrman, because of their ignorance, are not to blame for their misguided endeavors, the readers of *The Octopus* will be to blame if, having been instructed in the determinism of the social evils wrought by laissez faire economics, they continue to support a system whose outstanding feature is its tendency to bring unnecessary evil out of nature.

There remains to be considered the question of the soundness of the optimistic doctrine expressed at the very end of *The Octopus* by Presley:

> Falseness dies; injustice and oppression in the end of everything fade and vanish away. Greed, cruelty, selfishness, and inhumanity are short-lived; the individual suffers, but the race goes on. Annixter dies, but in a far distant corner of the world a thousand lives are saved. The larger view always and through all shams, all wickednesses, discovers the Truth that will, in the end, prevail, and all things, surely, inevitably, resistlessly work together for good.[22]

This doctine John Chamberlain condemns as "specious"[23] and Granville Hicks scorns as ridiculous."[24] Let us assume for the moment that the philosophy in question is "specious" and "ridiculous." It does not follow that Presley's conclusion is an utterance on which the philosophic reputations of Frank Norris and *The Octopus* must stand or fall. The conclusion is merely an observation on the way of the world from Presley's point of view, and Presley need not be regarded as Norris' *raisonneur*. An examination of Norris' comments on Presley's character shows clearly that Norris' respect for Presley's point of view was at best equivocal.

In the first chapter Norris remarks:

> One guessed that Presley's refinement had been gained only by a certain loss of strength. . . . It could be foreseen that morally he was of that sort who avoid evil through good taste, lack of decision, and want of opportunity. His temperament was that of the poet;

---

[22]*The Octopus*, p. 473.
[23]*Op. cit.*, pp. 105 and 107.
[24]*Op. cit.*, p. 173.

when he told himself he had been thinking, he deceived himself. He had, on such occasions, been only brooding.[25]

In the same chapter Norris asserts that Presley "wished to see everything through a rose-colored mist—a mist that dulled all harsh outlines, all crude and violent colors."[26] Then we read a few pages further on that "Presley was a confirmed dreamer, irresolute, inactive, with a strong tendency to melancholy. . . . . "[27]These descriptions of Presley make it obvious that Norris did not look upon this genteel eastern poet as a promising source of high philosophic truth.

But it makes little difference here whether we look upon Presley as Norris' *raisonneur* or not, for the conclusion of *The Octopus*— Presley's conclusion—is neither specious nor ridiculous. It is philosophically valid and is consistent, not only with Presley's character,[28] but also with Norris' whole conception of the novel with a purpose. Presley, it is true, might be incapable of defending logically his final optimism, for he has taken it at second hand from Vanamee not because he understands its implications but because it soothes his wounded emotions. But Norris would have no such difficulty. If Norris' premise—that the people, informed by the pulpit, the universities, and the novel, have the power to correct old errors and improve their society—if this be accepted (and those who reject such a premise reject simultaneously the thought of all perfectibilitarians from Rousseau to Franklin Delano Roosevelt), so also must the optimistic ending of *The Octopus* be accepted.

---

[25]*The Octopus*, p. 11.
[26]*Ibid.*, p. 14.
[27]*Ibid.*, p. 24.
[28]Similarly in character is Presley's final action in *The Octopus*. Like Étienne in Zola's *Germinal*, Presley is a developing character whose interpretation of the struggle he has witnessed and participated in is subject to change. Impressed first with the idea that the farmers might gain their ends by organized violence. Presley attempts to shape events by direct action —he tries to kill Behrman with Caraher's bomb—only to be frustrated by chance. Disillusioned and bewildered, Presley then turns to Shelgrim's view that nature is but a welter of brute forces indifferent to human purpose and that man can never improve his position in the meaningless animal struggle for existence. Finding this philosophy too shocking for comfort, Presley eagerly accepts the cheerful doctrine of the acknowledged mystic, Vanamee, and chooses to let others search for the truth and the good that will ultimately prevail. He himself books passage for India and escapes romantically from the scene of the disasters that have caused his distress. It is perhaps needless to remark that if Presley were meant to represent Norris consistently at the end of the book he would remain in America to write novels— or more poems—"with a Purpose."

The conclusion does not tell us, as John Chamberlain and Granville Hicks seem to think it does, that the truth has prevailed or that all things already have worked together for the good or that they now are working together for the good. The conclusion merely asserts that "the larger view always . . . . discovers the Truth that *will*, in the end, prevail, and all things, surely, inevitably, resistlessly work together for good." Not even Presley supposes that "Whatever is, is right."[29] He is well aware of the fact that neither the true nor the good has prevailed or is likely to prevail in a state controlled by the gigantic trust of the Pacific and Southwestern. Presley and Norris are optimistic only about the future, when sensitive poets will no longer flee to India for refuge from scenes of bloodshed and domestic disaster—when the novel with a purpose will have done its work and helped to establish throughout the world of men a society soundly based on potent nature and her perdurable laws.

---

[29]To conclude, as does H. Willard Reninger ("Norris Explains *The Octopus:* A Correlation of His Theory and Practice," *American Literature,* XII [May, 1940], 227) that the great truth disclosed by *The Octopus* is that "Whatever is, is right" is to suggest that Norris' knowledge of the history of philosophical speculation was limited to the lucubrations of such complacent thinkers as Leibnitz, Pope, and the memorable Dr. Pangloss. The truth is that the philosophy expressed by Norris through Vanamee and Presley in the latter pages of *The Octopus* compares favorably with the best naturalistic optimism available in America, England, and France at the close of the nineteenth century. This does not mean, however, that Norris was himself a great philosopher. In a later study I hope to show that both the philosophy and the plan of *The Octopus* originated not with Norris but with Émile Zola.

Lars Åhnebrink

From *The Beginnings of Naturalism in American Fiction*

The Octopus marks the beginning of a new phase in Norris's writings. His scope broadened and his concern was less with individual than with social problems. The change of attitude was partially due to his own maturity and his emerging interest in the conflicts and debates of his times, particularly between capital and labor, and between the plutocracy and the people. It must be remembered, however, that Norris was more interested in these conflicts and issues because they afforded material for dramatic stories than because he was concerned with reform and social justice. . . .

Although *The Octopus* contains many romantic elements, it is naturalistic in theme, treatment, and deterministic philosophy. It is a sociological novel which presents graphically the life and problems of the San Joaquin farmers, but Norris's attitude toward the issues involved is not consistent throughout the book. He sympathizes with the farmers and the 'reds,' but he finds excuses

Reprinted from Lars Åhnebrink *The Beginnings of Naturalism in American Fiction . . . 1891-1903,* [1950] (New York: Russell & Russell, 1961), 104-124, by permission of Russell & Russell, Publishers.

even for the railroad, a fact which somewhat disturbs the unity of the book, unless it is realized that Norris felt that both the railroad and its enemies were victims of forces they could not control. Norris's concern was primarily artistic and not ethical. (Cf. Garland's story "Under the Lion's Paw.") In the clash between the farmers and the railroad he saw mainly an issue of great dramatic quality, less a social evil which should be removed. Perhaps also an attempt at achieving objectivity and detachment had something to do with his apparently inconsistent attitude toward the problems involved.

. . . Granted its defects he considered it "a great book, simple, sombre, large, and of a final authority as the record of a tragical passage of American, or human events, which, if we did not stand in their every-day presence, we should shudder at as the presage of unexampled tyrannies."[1]

The Octopus contains some significant references to books and authors which may help us to understand certain aspects of the novel. Annixter now and then read a chapter of *David Copperfield*, and Magnus' wife enjoyed reading *Marius the Epicurean, The Essays of Elia, Sesame and Lilies,* and *The Stones of Venice.*[2] There are also references to Byron, Bryant, Goethe, Schiller, Bakunin, *Beowulf, The Nibelungen, The Roman de la Rose,* and Daudet's *Tartarin de Tarascon.* Judging from the following quotation it is probable that Norris had read some of the political and social thinkers of his day: Presley [read Norris] "flung aside his books of poems—Milton, Tennyson, Browning, even Homer— and addressed himself to Mill, Malthus, Young, Pushkin, Henry George, Schopenhauer."[3]

---

[1]"Editor's Easy Chair," *Harper's Monthly,* CIII (October, 1901), 825.
[2]*Compl. Works,* I, 57.
[3]*Ibid.,* II, 23.

Maxwell Geismar

From *Rebels and Ancestors*

Norris's young poet was to some extent a dupe of the epic of western life which he searched for. And what he found — the study of grain rates and freight tariffs — marked the history of Presley's (or Norris's own) emancipation from that rose-colored mist of romance which hovered over him. Very much like *The Grapes of Wrath* — whose direct predecessor *The Octopus* was in its drama of broad social conflict — the solid architecture of Norris's novel, the narrative structure, sustained the central story and gave it power even though separate elements in the tale are at first inadequate or histrionic. . . .

There were nice touches in the central love story of *The Octopus* when Annixter defended his character before the handsome and obdurate dairy maid. "I'm not such an entire swine to the people that know me — that jackass, Presley, for instance." When he proposes to her, we become aware of the degree to which Norris, for all his tendency to overdo his style, had developed a new western

Reprinted from *Rebels and Ancestors: The American Novel, 1890-1915* (New York: Hill and Wang, 1963), 1-66, by permission of the Houghton Mifflin Co. © 1953.

idiom, very different from the fine English of the universities and literary journals of the time. "You see, ever since the barn dance — yes, and long before then — I've been thinking a lot about you," Annixter says —

> "You're about the only girl that I ever knew well, and I guess . . . you're about the only one I want to know. It's my nature. . . . Why, if anything should happen to you, Miss Hilma — well, I wouldn't care to go on with anything. S. Behrman could jump Quien Sabe, and welcome. And Delaney could shoot me full of holes whenever he got good and ready. I'd quit. I'd lay right down. I wouldn't care a whoop about anything any more. You are the only girl for me in the whole world."

It was a declaration of passion that described the behavior of the western male in many later American novels, and, as the love affair reached a climax, the economic and social drama filled the novel's stage. Probably Norris as yet lacked the imaginative capacity of such writers as Melville and Dreiser to convert the raw materials of an industry or an economic system into poetry of the highest order; but here too *The Octopus* improved upon itself and discovered its own way as one of the earliest American novels to describe the technics of monopoly capitalism in its grand period. The early episode of the plows which were shipped through San Joaquin Valley to Los Angeles, and then shipped back by the Pacific and Southwestern at short-haul (higher) rates, gave the key to this story of economic exploitation and the linked strategies of finance and politics in modern society. When Dyke, the black-listed railroad engineer, discovers that the freight rate for hops has been changed without notice, he asks S. Behrman, "Yes, what's your rule? What's your basis?" in a sharp episode. "All-the-traffic-will-bear," the district representative of the railroad repeats. (The meaning of Norris's tag-names became clear here, and perhaps this was one source of the wild barbaric yawp of the immigrant names in *The Financier* and *The Titan* as later epics of finance capitalism.)

The unifying concept of the novel was of course that of a whole new society, barely established on the western frontier of the democracy, whose most representative functions and institutions were already controlled by the monopoly. And the course of the slippery negotiations — the tactics of deception, the technics of corruption—which followed invariably in the wake, or the slough, of the railroad corporation was admirably treated in *The Octopus.*...

There were still faults of technique in these pages. Norris's penchant for melodrama led him to raise the account of Dyke's crime and capture into another Wild West saga. Lurid, too, in terms of wanton bloodshed and violence was the big scene in which 'the forces of law and order' (the railroad) took over the ranchers' land and were opposed by force. In which argument led to rifle fire — a blundering, uncertain, improvised battle where all the plans of the ranchers were overturned and Annixter, Harran Derrick, the cowboy Delaney, the Dutch farmer Hooven, the ridiculous Osterman—"this poser, this silly fellow, this cracker of jokes, whom no one had ever taken very seriously" — were killed. Yet, even here, the often brilliant strokes of organization and exposition that lay beneath the overheated prose, and the passages of pure carnage, carried the story along. . . .

And when Norris's young observer reached the general offices of the railroad and met Shelgrim himself, the master financier who was based on the character of Collis Huntington, was he really so swayed by the power and eloquence of the Superman of Transportation? The argument was that of classical economics within the framework of the new Darwinism: the law of the jungle adapted to the uses of capitalism. "Forces, conditions, laws of supply and demand — were these then the enemy after all?" Nature had become merely "a leviathan with a heart of steel," formed in the image of the locomotive engine, rather than the self-regulating mechanism, the watch or clock of eighteenth century Deism. And the Lord himself, who had opened his career as the Cosmic Shepherd of the Hebrew tribes, had the appearance of a frustrated engineer. Yet, though earlier studies of *The Octopus* have stressed this phase of Norris's thinking, one notices the prevailing imagery in the portrait of Shelgrim: the skullcap, the frock coat, the pale blue eyes which give the impression of a spider at the very center of the web. And the name. When Norris's hero was confronted by the signs of "an opulence so great that it need never be husbanded" in the house of the railroad magnate Girard, he reflects that, after all, it was the farmers who paid for it.

"It was for this that S. Behrman turned the screw, tightened the vise. It was for this that Dyke had been driven to outlawry and a jail. It was for this that Lyman Derrick had been bought, the Governor ruined and broken, Annixter shot, Hooven killed." While the hors d'oeuvres were being served with wine from southern France at this magnificent dinner party, and outside the rancher Hooven's wife and child wander homeless in the streets, the poet

Presley has a sudden fantasy that all his friends were being eaten by these glittering society women amidst the chased silver, Dresden crockery and cut-glass dishes; that in a sort of unspeakable cannibalism they were all being devoured there under his eyes. "These dainty women . . . frail, delicate; all these fine ladies with their small fingers and slender necks, suddenly were transfigured in his tortured mind into harpies tearing human flesh."

The intellectual climax of the novel was here; afterwards there was the famous scene where S. Behrman, caught by accident in the hold of a ship which was being filled by his new grain elevator, was smothered beneath the pouring mass of wheat, his cries lost in the metallic roar, his death slow and cruel. . . . . And this was a long step from our first glimpse of Norris's young spokesman, who very much like the early heroes of John Dos Passos and the esthetic novelists of the 1920's, had dreamed about the "desire of creation" while he read his little tree-calf edition of the *Odyssey*. "Reality was what he longed for. . . . Yet how to make this compatible with romance?" the novelist said about this protagonist; but Norris himself had come to realize that it was a naïve sense of romance, a narrow sense of reality.

. . . The later sections of the novel are an admirable description of the western fortunes at home where we feel that the novelist really had begun both to understand the inner workings of his society and to describe them in bold and original terms. Despite obvious failings which we usually accept in any work of real character, after all, and which in the end we may come to cherish in a talent that transcends its limitations, *The Octopus* was a major achievement of Norris's and another landmark in early twentieth century realism . . . .

Donald Pizer

Another Look at
The Octopus

Many critics of American literature have admired the breadth
and vitality of Frank Norris' *The Octopus*. Most of these same
critics have also pointed out what they consider grave philosophical
inconsistencies in the novel. Walter F. Taylor finds that Norris varies
between the value of free will and determinism. Ernest Marchand
notes that he "wavers between the idea of impersonal force for
which good and evil have no meaning and the idea of a triumphant
good for which the universe itself stands sponsor." The close of the
novel has been particularly attacked. V. L. Parrington considers
that in it Norris abandons an amoral attitude and takes refuge in
a moral order. Charles C. Walcutt regards it as an appeasement of
the emotions in which "the thoughtful reader is bound after a time
to feel that . . . he . . . has been swindled of a solution."[1]

© 1955 by The Regents of the University of California. Reprinted from
Nineteenth-Century Fiction, X, 217-224, by permission of The Regents.

[1]Walter F. Taylor, *The Economic Novel in America* (Chapel Hill, N. C.,
1942), p. 299; Ernest Marchand, *Frank Norris: A Study* (Stanford University,
1942), p. 81; Vernon L. Parrington, *Main Currents in American Thought*
(New York, 1930), III, 333; Charles C. Walcutt, "Frank Norris and the
Search for Form," *University of Kansas City Review,* XIV (Winter, 1947),
135.

I wish to show that much of this criticism of *The Octopus* results from a lack of understanding of Norris' handling of Presley, one of the chief characters in the novel. It is important to note that most critics identify Presley's pronouncements with Norris. Robert E. Spiller, who makes many of the above objections, states that Norris had no consistent position, for he "shifts with his poet Presley from . . . mechanistic determinism to mystical theism and back." Marchand regards him as a "vehicle of the author's emotions and ideas." Taylor presents clearly this conception of the misleading quality of Presley: that "the reader, who has received so much of the story through the medium of Presley's earlier, moral point of view, is nowhere prepared for this sudden change of front, so that the large optimism of the concluding pages . . . has . . . the disconcerting effect of a verdict given against the evidence."[2]

I

The heart of the novel lies in Norris' similar development of three major characters, the poet Presley, the rancher Annixter, and the ascetic shepherd Vanamee. In all three the process is one of achieving a "larger view," that is, a casting aside of personal values and the attainment of a philosophical perspective. By this means Presley learns the truth of good and evil, Annixter of love, and Vanamee of life and death. In all three this is acomplished by an imaginative and emotional reliance upon self in the presence of nature, with nature—through the symbol of the wheat—acting as both a guide and a confirmation of the truth thus discovered.

For Presley the process is a gradual one. At the opening of the novel he is characterized as an overrefined poet searching for the True Romance, an epic theme upon which to write his great poem of the West. On a slope overlooking many miles of the rich San Joaquin he gazes out over the bare, harvested fields, seeing in them "his epic, his inspiration, his West."[3] But at this time Presley's "morbid supersensitive mind" cannot grasp the meaning of the scene, and "terrible, formless shapes, vague figures . . . whirled at a gallop through his imagination" (I, 44). But he proceeds no further, for there is a violent interruption as a crack railroad

[2]*Literary History of the United States,* ed. Robert E. Spiller *et al.* (New York, 1948), II, 1033; Marchand, p. 145; Taylor, p. 299.
[3]*The Complete Works of Frank Norris* (Garden City, N.Y., 1928), I, 44. Citations hereafter appear in the text.

engine plows into a herd of sheep which had wandered onto a nearby track. "The inspiration vanished like a mist," and, in the oft-repeated epithets, Presley characterizes the railroad as "the soulless Force, the iron-hearted Power, the monster, the Colossus, the Octopus" (I, 48).

Presley is soon drawn into the wheat growers' struggle against the railroad. It is immediately after a meeting at which their League discovers that it has been betrayed to the railroad that he again perceives the wheat, this time the young wheat growing in the night. He realizes now that it is "indifferent, gigantic, resistless," that "Men . . . were born . . . died, and were forgotten; while the Wheat . . . grew steadily under the night . . . " (II, 161). But the fight at the irrigation ditch and the death of his friends shake Presley out of any equilibrium this realization might have given him. Under the impact of the personal tragedies evolving from the fight he is overcome by a "sombre brooding malevolence" and after making an impassioned speech attacking the railroad, attempts to kill the local railroad agent.

A month later, in San Francisco, he is yet filled with a "spirit of unrest and revolt." On a whim he approaches Shelgrim, the president of the railroad. He lectures Presley: "You are dealing with forces . . . when you speak of Wheat and the Railroads, not with men"; therefore "Blame conditions, not men" (II, 285) is the crux of his argument. To Presley, this "rang with the clear reverberation of truth." He now conceives of nature in terms of a "Colossal indifference only, a vast trend toward appointed goals. Nature was, then, a gigantic engine, a vast Cyclopean power . . . " (II, 286). But despite its "truth" there is for Presley no satisfaction in this knowledge.[4] Soon he discovers that Shelgrim's concept of force is inadequate, that he is yet concerned with individuals: "The Railroad might indeed be a force only, which no man could control and for which no man was responsible, but his friends had been killed . . . " (II, 317).

Before leaving for India, Presley returns to the San Joaquin, to the scene of his first awareness of the wheat, and again views the bare fields, the cycle of growth now completed. He now realizes "strong and true the sense and significance of all the enigma of growth" and seems "for one instant to touch the explanation of existence." For he perceives that "Men were naught, death was naught, life was naught; FORCE only existed . . . " (II, 343).

---

[4]Cf. the similarity in epithets between Presley's initial characterization of the railroad (I, 48) and the characterization he is forced to draw of nature (II, 286) because of Shelgrim's "truth."

Each succeeding perception of the wheat by Presley had meant an increase in knowledge. His first perception, on this same slope, had resulted in vagueness. The second, after the League meeting, terminated in an awareness of the power of nature, the insignificance of man. This was strengthened by Shelgrim's concept of force. But Shelgrim's force was essentially negative—something to blame—and still did not quiet Presley's unrest.

Each previous perception had been vitiated by events concerning individuals. But now, instead of the slaughter of sheep[5] or a massacre at an irrigation ditch, Vanamee, the ascetic shepherd, appears with a theory of good and evil based on his own realization of truth. If "your view be large enough," he tells Presley, you will find that "it is *not* evil, but good, that in the end remains" (II, 345).

The ship on which Presley leaves for India is loaded with grain for the relief of an Indian famine. As Presley muses over the personal tragedies of the ranchers, Vanamee's words return to him, and Norris presents Presley's final drawing of knowledge from the wheat, this time the wheat in the hold beneath his feet:

> *But the* WHEAT *remained.* Untouched, unassailable, undefiled, that mighty world-force . . . moved onward in its appointed grooves. Through the welter of blood at the irrigating ditch . . . the great harvest of Los Muertos rolled like a flood from the Sierras to the Himalayas to feed thousands of starving scarecrows on the barren plains of India.
>
> . . . Annixter dies, but in a far-distant corner of the world a thousand lives are saved. The larger view always and through all shams, all wickedness, discovers the Truth that will, in the end, prevail, and all things, surely, inevitably, resistlessly work together for good (II, 360-361).

II

As Presley realizes the "larger view" and therefore Truth, so do Annixter and Vanamee. For them, however, the process is compressed into one sharp and dramatic realization.

Annixter is initially characterized as a rough, self-centered, intolerant man, "widely hated." He attempts to fight off his love for Hilma Tree, a pretty milkmaid, but is unable to do so. His clumsy attempt to kiss her, and his clumsier proposal for an illicit

---

[5]In its foreshadowing, symbolic sense the sheep massacre obviously represents "individuals" as much as the later fight at the irrigation ditch.

relationship repel the girl, though she loves him, and she runs
off to San Francisco. When he discovers Hilma is gone, Annixter
wanders out into the wheat fields and mulls over the problem. His
"imagination, unused, unwilling machine, began to work." Realizing the selfishness of his attitude toward love, "By a supreme
effort, not of the will, but of the emotion, he fought his way across
that vast gulf that for a time had gaped between Hilma and the
idea of his marriage" (II, 80-81).

At this moment Annixter notices the young wheat in the early
morning light and identifies the wheat as a benevolent life force
with love as a benevolent life force: "There it was, the Wheat,
the Wheat!" Like his realization of the Truth of love, it too had
just emerged, and so "Once more the strength of nations was re-
newed. Once more the force of the world was revivified" (II, 82-83).

When Presley encounters Vanamee at the opening of the novel
he learns of Vanamee's tragic past, of his love many years earlier
for Angèle, who had been raped and had died in childbirth. Vanamee's face is "stamped with an unspeakable sadness, a deathless
grief," and he is a man "whose life had suddenly stopped at a certain moment of its development" (I, 32). In a paroxysm of grief
he attempts to use his strange hypnotic power of attracting people
to call the dead Angèle to him. He receives a faint "Answer," an
impulse in return, and soon is haunting the mission garden where
this had occurred, striving to call forth Angèle completely. On
the same night of Annixter's experience on the edge of the wheat
field Vanamee, "dizzied with mysticism," his imagination "reshap-
ing itself," feels the "Answer" very close. It appears, and though
he learns it is not Angèle, but rather her daughter, he is yet
exultant:

> Angèle or Angèle's daughter, it was all one with him. It was She.
> Death was overcome. The grave vanquished. Life, ever-renewed,
> alone existed. Time was naught; change was naught; all things were
> immortal but evil; all things eternal but grief.

At this moment he notices the wheat:

> There it was. The Wheat! The Wheat! In the night it had come
> up. . . . Once more the pendulum of the seasons swung in its mighty
> arc, from death back to life. Life out of death, eternity rising from
> out dissolution. There was the lesson (II, 106).

III

The way is now clear for an examination of the charges that Norris was confused by the distinction between a moral and an amoral world, and that he was also confused in dealing with free will and determinism. The belief that he dawdled between a moral and an amoral world stems primarily from a lack of understanding of Presley's role as a developing character, and the frequent assumption that Presley's thoughts represent Norris himself. For example, Marchand maintains that Norris was in error, for he could "conclude *The Octopus* with the assertion that 'all things . . . work together for good,' and at the same time proclaim that the universe was neither benign nor malevolent, that 'FORCE only existed.'[6] The point is that throughout the novel Presley progresses toward his ultimate perception of Truth. It is the various stages in the development of Presley which cause confusion. It is not Norris who varies between the idea of impersonal force and triumphant good, but Presley. And Norris does not "shift with his poet Presley," but rather represents Presley's gradual and much troubled progression toward Truth. Presley's preoccupation with individual tragedy and his personal involvement hinder him from achieving the "larger view." This constitutes his earlier, moral attitude. However, led by his perception of the wheat and Shelgrim, he formulates an amoral, impersonal conception of force. But again this does not answer his doubts. It is only with the return to a moral attitude, but now on a "cosmic" level, that he achieves the "larger view" and Truth. The representation, then, of any of Presley's earlier generalizations as Norris', no matter how true they seemed to Presley at the time, is false in the light of what Norris had ultimately in mind for Presley.[7]

---

[6]Marchand, p. 87.

[7]There is an understandable reason for mistaking the earlier Presley for Norris. Any critic of Norris immediately recognizes many of Presley's views on literature and art as those of Norris, and therefore tends to equate Presley's other pronouncements with Norris also. But if only Presley's final realization represents Norris, George W. Meyer inquires ("A New Interpretation of *The Octopus,*" *College English,* IV [March, 1943], 359n), why is he escaping to India rather than remaining to write literature with a purpose? However, Presley as a poet is characterized as too "literary" and as incapable of reaching the People. He is a failure in his attempt to aid the ranchers despite his success in "The Toilers." This dual aspect of Presley does not mean he cannot achieve Truth, just as Annixter had achieved it despite his ill-fated role in the League.

The investigation of Norris' treatment of free will and determinism does reveal, however, a dichotomy in his mind, that of free
will on the personal level—leading to both good and evil—and
optimistic determinism on the "cosmic" level. For the ranchers,
Magnus Derrick, Dyke, and the others, are not simply the victims
of economic determinism most writers like to consider them. They
are just as much the victims of their own business inability, as
Dyke, or gambling nature, as Magnus, or general lack of alertness
and preparedness, as all the ranchers. And both Vanamee and Annixter exert free will in leading a better life due to their realization
of Truth.[8] But, in contrast to these cases of individual responsibility, the final Truth of Presley conceives of the world in terms
of optimistic determinism, that "all things . . . inevitably, resistlessly work together for good." Obviously the two—freedom on
the personal level, determinism on the "cosmic"—are not incompatible in Norris' mind, and he would feel no need to resolve them.

The most striking aspects of the novel, in view of the usual
placing of Norris at the head of American naturalism, are Norris'
treatment of the derivation of Truth and his conception of the
quality of nature. It is revealing to contrast Norris' presentation
of the correct method of arriving at truth with that used by Zola
in *Germinal*, a novel Norris knew well and which is frequently
mentioned as a source for *The Octopus*.[9] Etienne, like Presley,
serves as a focusing point in an economic dispute. His arrival on
the scene begins the novel, his departure ends it, and much of the
novel is concerned with his activities in relation to the dispute. But
the conclusions reached by Etienne when "his education was complete"[10] are derived empirically. The means which had been used
by the miners—force and violence—were not the best, and had resulted in failure. Another method—that of quiet organization—
would perhaps be to more advantage. On the other hand, Annixter,
Vanamee, and Presley all rely upon themselves in their imaginative

---

[8]Annixter, with his new conception of the value and meaning of love, soon wins
Hilma and begins treating his fellowmen with kindness and sympathy, Vanamee, perceiving the true nature of life and death, discards his selfish grief and
accepts life and reality in the form of Angèle's daughter.

[9]Lars Åhnebrink, *The Beginning of Naturalism in American Fiction* (Cam-
bridge, Mass. 1950), pp. III, 294-298.

[10]Émile Zola, *Germinal,* trans. Havelock Ellis (New York, 1937), p. 469.

and emotional capacity to perceive the "larger view" and Truth, this with the aid of a didactic and benevolent nature.[11]

The Octopus, then, with all its relationship to contemporary interests, both in theories of fiction and social affairs, in at least two important ways is looking backward rather than forward in its relationship to American thought, since Norris' faith in individual perception of Truth and in the concomitant dependence upon a benevolent nature in discerning this Truth found its most distinct statement in the transcendental movement.

---

[11]Norris' belief in nature's didacticism has been frequently overlooked. A further example of this belief is his conception of the artist returning from nature "to the world of men with a true-beating heart, and a true-hearing ear, so that he understands once more . . . , and the Man writes true and clear, and his message rings with harmony and with melody, with power and with passion of the prophets interpreting God's handwriting to the world of men." (*The Responsibilities of the Novelist* [New York, 1903], pp. 276-277.)

Charles Child Walcutt

From *American Literary Naturalism*

... It is clear. ... that *The Octopus* is in the naturalistic tradition in its delineation of the broad sweep of economic forces. It is naturalistic in the Zola tradition, and its qualities may be further elucidated by comparison with those of Zola's novel which it most closely resembles, *Germinal*.

The most striking quality that the two works have in common is the epic sweep. ...

... [For] it must be observed that if [the] similarities represent an influence of Zola upon Norris it is a literary influence, a matter of method, of storytelling, that has no necessary relation to the philosophy of naturalism.

More interesting and fruitful are the dissimilarities between these novels, for it is through them that Norris's position in the naturalistic movement may be explained. The most important problem in the consideration of any panoramic naturalistic novel is the relation between the characters and the external forces that oppress or control them, the amount of will displayed, and the extent to which such "will" is explained in terms of the forces which the novel presents. In *Germinal*, it will be recalled, the mine has made the miners what they are, has determined their economic situation and physical characteristics from generation to generation. During the action of the novel it pervades and directs their thoughts. It is the object against which they struggle even while it is responsible for having made them what they are. No two characters can affect each other without the mine's having some part in their activity. Physically and spiritually ubiquitous, it is a force with amazing power and scope of operation.

In *The Octopus* conditions are otherwise. The characters begin their struggle with the Trust as free, ethical, and independent men who have achieved a high degree of prosperity upon the frontier. They have struggled with nature and triumphed. And the struggle of such titans with the Octopus is Homeric in conception rather than a pathetic illustration of determining forces controlling helpless and insignificant automata. Annixter is the most striking example of an heroic frontiersman. He is a despiser of "feemale girls," a distruster of marriage, hot-tempered, contentious, gruffly generous. He calls his enemy a *pip*, eats quantities of dried prunes, and re-reads *David Copperfield* constantly. He is college educated, and his ranch is a model of efficiency and modern brightness. Considerable attention is given to his romance with Hilma Tree, who works for him: "Annixter turned into the dairy-house . . . Hilma stood bathed from head to foot in the torrent of sunlight that poured in upon her from the three wide-open windows. She was charming, delicious, radiant of youth, of health, of well-being." He intrudes upon her innocence by a clumsy attempt to kiss her, is properly mortified at his own gaucherie, and stamps off in a rage. But the seed is planted, the hater of women is trapped. It is some time before he can accept the idea of love, and, above all, marriage. Finally he drives her from him, but an all-night vigil under the stars shows him the way:

> By a supreme effort, not of the will, but of the emotion, he fought his way across that vast gulf that for a time had gaped between Hilma and the idea of his marriage. Instantly, like the swift blending of beautiful colours, like the harmony of beautiful chords of music, the two ideas melted into one, and in that moment into his harsh, unlovely world a new idea was born. Annixter stood suddenly upright, a mighty tenderness, a gentleness of spirit, such

as he has never conceived of, in his heart strained, swelled, and in a moment seemed to burst. Out of the dark furrows of his soul, up from the deep rugged recesses of his being, something rose, expanding . . .
"Why . . . I *love* her," he cried.

These activities enhance Annixter's personal independence. They add "spiritual" elements to his character that defy explanation in terms of heredity and environment. His stature is further increased by a duel which he has with a discharged farm hand who dashes on horseback into the dance that Annixter is giving in honor of his new barn. Firing blindly through the smoke, Annixter is astonished to discover that he has hit his opponent in the hand:

> "Well, where did *you* learn to shoot *that way?*" someone in the crowd demanded. Annixter moved his shoulders with a gesture of vast unconcern.
> "Oh," he observed carelessly, "it's not my *shooting* that ever worries *me,* m'son."
> The crowd gaped with delight. There was a great wagging of heads.

Such offhanded, humorous bravado takes us out of the feeling of a confined, determined life. This same freedom becomes headstrong defiance when the Railroad serves, an hour later, its notice of the new land prices. The ranchers' league is formed in an explosion of defiance. Knowing the power of the Railroad, the reader will regard this event as tragic irony rather than as an illustration of economic determinism. Annixter's death at the climax is tragically wasteful but also heroic. It is almost a glorious death. . . .

The . . . difference of conception between the *Octopus* and *Germinal* extends to the very symbols which the two authors employ. The Octopus, as we have seen, is an actively evil and malignant force. Adjectives like "inexorable," "iron-hearted," and "pitiless" are constantly applied to it. It is cruel and villainous—a thing to be hated. Compare with this the mine buildings and the black tower of the Voreux in *Germinal.* Gloomy, black, immobile, they stand as a symbol of oppression. But no false attempt is made to have them reach out and devour the miners. Instead they squat there as gaunt and horrible symbols of the forces which the miners cannot evade. Their immobility makes them ideally representative of the economic forces which dominate the book. No moral values can be attached to them; they do not indulge in active evil for which they can be hated. They represent the nature of deterministic forces—inescapable, unchanging, destroyed only by the earthshaking catastrophe of revolution or the destructive anarchy of

Souverine who lets in the water that floods the mine and swallows up the buildings. Zola's symbol carries philosophical as well as dramatic significance. Norris's is almost solely dramatic. . . .

Here, then, is where the fabric of reason is thinnest in *The Octopus*. The wheat as an incarnation of natural dynamism, of an inherent desire in nature to be bountiful, is equated with the prevailing social arrangements for buying and selling. Laissez-faire economics is treated as if it were an aspect of nature's dynamic urge to reproduce herself and feed her children. We are told that *how* the wheat is distributed does not matter; we are almost persuaded that the manner of its distribution is a part of nature's larger plan. One does not of course question a novelist's right to accept laissez-faire economics. But we must note that these conclusions do not satisfactorily answer the *problem as posed* in the novel. That problem is not whether the wheat will finally be eaten (it always was in those days) but whether the railroads must and will continue to swindle and oppress the less powerful American citizens whom, if the will of our democracy is to find expression, it is supposed to serve in a free market. The question is whether the people must or should stand for such criminal injustice, whether our social order must countenance a condition in which a corporation controls the press, the banks, and the courts and so becomes a law unto itself in defiance of democratic process. This problem is not solved. It is simply evaded, while a vaguely religious affirmation of ultimate good is offered to appease the emotions aroused by the action.

When Behrman, the immediate individual object of the reader's dislike, is smothered in the hold of the wheat ship, pent-up emotions are released. The reader is made to feel, by this poetic fusion of disparate elements, that the wheat as a force has answered the social and economic problem of the novel, the problem of monopoly and coercion. Of course it has not, and the thoughtful reader is bound after a time to feel that it is he who has been swindled of a solution. Conditions in the American West differed essentially from those in the coal mines of *Germinal* where there was no answers for either miner or owner. Zola was true to his materials and wove a consistently dark tragic pattern—leaving at the end a single bright thread in the suggestion that revolution must inevitably come. Norris copies this tragic pattern for a conflict that did not have to end tragically. The democratic process could still work in America, where there were natural resources in abundance and relatively few people. Not revolution but a safer legal basis for trade was indicated. The tragedy of the story speaks magnificently for itself. It is the attempt to explain it that does irreparable harm to the novel. Only once is there a strong expression of the new naturalistic philosophy, when Presley ponders the idea of a mechanistic universe, indifferent and unchangeable, which pursues its way not toward the utilitarian goal of prosperity but toward no goal at all, operating merely because motion is the law of the cosmic mechanism:

> Nature was, then, a gigantic engine, a vast Cyclopean power, huge, terrible, a leviathan with a heart of steel, knowing no compunction, no forgiveness, no tolerance; crushing out the human atom standing in its way with nirvanic calm, the agony of destruction sending never a jar, never the faintest tremor through all that prodigious mechanism of wheels and cogs.[22]

One is tempted to perceive a close relationship between the incoherence of Norris's philosophy and the steadily growing orotundity of his style. In *The Octopus* there is an endless accumulation of sonorous adjectives. The rolling periods throb and rumble. Sometimes they produce superb effects; at other times they seem rather to be giving voice to a love of power and size which, an end in itself, sweeps careful ratiocination aside. Norris's development thus far shows a steady movement toward this love of high-sounding words. As the style inflates, the conviction of his books diminishes. *McTeague,* though better built, carries less final conviction than *Vandover. The Octopus,* still better constructed, has less than *McTeague.*

But in the last analysis *The Octopus* is one of the finest American novels written before 1910. It towers immeasurably far above the sickly sentiment of Norris's contemporaries. Its chief weakness can be traced to a certain feebleness of intellectual grip, and this feebleness is reflected in the inadequacy of his grasp on the ideology —naturalism—through which he chose to work. It must be emphasized that he does not fall short merely because he was not a perfect naturalist, but because of the intellectual softness which prevented him from completely mastering the set of ideas he adopted. We may assume that he would have similarly failed in the comprehension of another philosophy that required the same sharpness of perception. We may, further, conclude that the naturalistic philosophy provided a much-needed discipline for Norris's creative exuberance—a discipline which aided him wonderfully in directing his genius toward expression in significant form. As the tonic effect of this discipline abated, Norris went over toward the trifling contemporaries whom he had previously condemned. . . .

---

[22]*Ibid.,* II, 286. Oddly enough, this passage follows right after Shelgrim's explanation that "the Wheat will be carried to feed the people."

Richard Chase

From *The American Novel and Its Tradition*

... The most appealing character in the novel, and the only one who is developed novelistically, so that we understand the inner strains of the man and can carefully watch the changes that take place in him, is another rancher named Annixter. He is a brilliant, irritable man with chronic indigestion who eats prunes all day and is reading *David Copperfield* throughout *The Octopus*. He is a maverick, a cynic, and has a raw, distrustful contempt for human beings. He is a strong woman-hater but is finally brought out of his misanthropy by his love for Hilma Tree, a kind of Eternal Woman or Goddess of the Wheat who works in Annixter's dairy. Through his love for her he is newly made a member of the human race, before being killed in an encounter with the marshal and the railroad agents. The story of Annixer and Hilma Tree departs from the canons of naturalism—according to which any character involved in life must degenerate in a straight line of descent and defeat. A tragic note is struck in his humanization and subsequent death, and his life is implied to be a kind of triumph, rather than just another bleak and meaningless episode in the spectacle of human fate, which is the usual impression Norris leaves about the meaning of individual lives. . . .

Then there is Vanamee, a character on whom the author seems to bank rather heavily as a representative of the mysterious and occult branches of experience. . . .

. . . He finally finds peace of mind in the Christian-pagan message that may be derived from the book—namely that death, injustice, and suffering are redeemed and recompensed in the eternal rebirth of Life, symbolized by the cycle of the wheat.

But much the most portentous character in *The Octopus* is Presley, who is in an odd way one side of Norris himself and who acts fitfully as the book's center of intelligence. Presley is rather abstractly conceived as a poet and an intellectual. In keeping with the clichés of lowbrow literature, which *The Octopus* is, he is presented as *the* poet, *the* intellectual. It seems clear that in the figure of Presley, Norris is shriving himself of one aspect of his own personality—for he too was a poet and intellectual or might have been had he not escaped the early influences of his education in France and at Harvard. . . .

Norris thus makes out of Presley a prototype of a whole series of "intellectuals" and "poets" who are imagined in modern liberal idealism to have given up literature for political action or for a closer contact with reality, because of their sense of social injustice and their perception of the impotence of literature to affect the reality into which they try to hurl themselves. Presley seems, however, to be operating in a vacuum; for he never has any real involvement with or knowledge of either literature or politics. Perhaps we may call Presley a subintellectual, as his friend Vanamee is a submystic. This is nothing against them—the only point being that Norris takes each of them for the genuine article.

Although Vanamee finds a religious significance in the life cycle of the wheat, Norris himself derives a different lesson and the book concludes with a declaration of the naturalist creed. . . . It is possible to suppose momentarily that Norris is presenting something like Henry Adams's symbolic Virgin and Dynamo. The Wheat, that is, might be the benignant nourishing force which in the end overcomes the inhuman and destructive force symbolized by the railroad. But in Norris's mind there is no differentiation of forces; there is only Force, and although *The Octopus* seems to be a liberal diatribe against capitalist reaction, the railroad and every injustice it brings with it, down to the last foreclosure on the most miserable property, are finally said to be as exempt from moral evaluation as the wheat itself. Both are irresistible manifestations of the "world-force." This irrationalism comes into play, however, only when Norris is trying to make ultimate formulations or when he breaks over into his particular kind of impassioned poetic insight (the same may be said of other naturalistic writers, particularly Norris's fellow Californians Jack London and Robinson Jeffers).

There is thus all through his work a tension between Norris the liberal humanist and ardent democrat and Norris the proto-fascist, complete with a racist view of Anglo-Saxon supremacy, a myth of the superman, and a portentous nihilism (some of Norris's anti-intellectual and reactionary views seem to have been derived from reading Kipling and from misreading Nietzsche, as well as from nativist sources). By way of contrast one might recall the more sympathetic view of Melville who shares Norris's love of the sheer poetry of power and death. At the end of *The Octopus* we are left to contemplate an irresistible force which supposedly works for "good"—but for the good of whom or what? is it the "human swarm"?—whereas in *Moby-Dick* we are left with Ishmael on the coffin-lifebuoy, a man in his plight as an individual....

... In *The Octopus* we find a full use of the conspiracy theory of history—the theory that all would be well with American life if only it were not for the machinations of the money power—the bankers, the railroad magnates, and their panoply of venal journalists and lawyers, suborned marshals, and hired assassins.

The main difference between the folklore of Populism and the imagination of Frank Norris is that naturalist doctrine has given him an underlying pessimism about nature itself and man's place in it. Norris appears to accept what Mr. Hofstadter calls "the concept of natural harmonies," a utopian faith in the natural order and in the virtue of man's living in harmony with it; but this view of things always has to contend in Norris's mind with a radically pessimistic view. As with most American naturalistic novelists, the pessimism wins out in the end, but in doing so it seems to take over from the idyl of nature some of its poetic, utopian quality, so that what we have is not hardheaded Darwinism but romantic nihilism, the final implication of which is that death itself is utopia.

Norris's romance-novels succeeded in reclaiming for American fiction an imaginative profundity that the age of Howells was leaving out—a fact which Norris's crudity and passages of bad writing cannot conceal. *McTeague* introduced to the novel a new animal vitality and a new subject matter drawn from lower-class life. From a moral and intellectual point of view, *The Octopus* has to be called a sort of subnovel. Yet no sympathetic reader can forget its enormous panoramic power. The book has, as D. H. Lawrence says, a brooding, primitive tone, an astonishing sense of a world instinct with sinister forces, that remind one of Cooper's *The Prairie*.

In view of their imaginative achievement one does not worry too much, in reading Norris's books, about their sentence-to-sentence faults of syntax and language, although like Dreiser, Norris was unable to tell whether the English he himself wrote was good or bad. *McTeague* and *The Octopus* prove again that it is possible to master certain fundamental aspects of the art of prose fiction despite the imperfection of the language in which the feat is achieved. . . .

Donald Pizer

The Concept of Nature in
Frank Norris' *The Octopus*

Perhaps I should immediately explain that the term "Nature" in my title has little to do with the Zolaesque naturalism that conventionally serves as the basis for discussion of Norris' ideas. Rather, my thesis is that *The Octopus* is best explicated by examining it within the context of the late nineteenth-century American attempt to reconcile evolutionary science and religious faith. I hope to prove that the guiding system of ideas in the novel is an evolutionary theism which attributes to nature the powers and qualities usually assigned to a personal, supernatural deity. An understanding of this system is important because it frees the novel from its traditional charge of philosophical inconsistency, and because it indicates the native intellectual roots of a writer usually considered to be a prime example of foreign indebtedness.

First, a few words about evolutionary theism in late nineteenth-century America.[1] There were perhaps two major ways in which

Reprinted from *American Quarterly* XIV (Spring 1962), 73-80, by permission of University of Pennsylvania. Copyright, 1962, Trustees of the University of Pennsylvania.
[1]General discussions of the movement are: Herbert W. Schneider, *A History of American Philosophy* (New York, 1946), pp. 321-80 and Stow Persons, "Evolution and Theology in America," in *Evolutionary Thought in America,* ed. Stow Persons (New Haven, 1950), pp. 422-53.

Christian evolutionists, as they were often called, attempted to reconcile evolution and religion. The first, and by far the more conventional and popular, was to assign to God the traditional role of first cause or designer—His was the master hand which had devised or was guiding the eternal processes of change. Natural law was therefore divine law, and since the evolution of man's soul was God's primary intent, man was returned to the center of the world's stage, and order, symmetry and direction were reestablished in comic affairs. The second method of reconciliation derived from Herbert Spencer, and was more radical, since it came perilously close to the heresy of pantheism. Spencer, arguing from the law of the conservation of energy, claimed that the basic constituent of the universe was force, though this force of energy took the correlated forms of matter, motion, space and time. Evolution, to Spencer, was the universal process of change caused by the omnipresence and persistence of force. Though Spencer was an agnostic, a number of his disciples immediately recognized the possibility of identifying force with divine energy—that is, to attribute to God not only the function of first cause, but also of immanence in nature and in nature's processes and laws. Such an identification was particularly attractive to those who desired to reinvest nature with the qualities of a benevolent and apprehendable divinity, qualities which it appeared to have been deprived of by the initial shock of Darwinism.

American evolutionary theism, however, incorporated not only a teleology, but also an epistemology and an ethic. The epistemology leaned sharply toward the transcendental, since American liberal theology, from whose camp most evolutionary theists derived, still contained a powerful vestige of transcendentalism. Indeed, the idea of immanence was strikingly congenial to those trancendentally inclined, for immanence suggested the possibility of an immediate, intuitive perception of the divine knowledge present in nature.[2] Evolutionary theistic ethics, besides containing a number of traditional explanations of evil, moved in a somewhat new direction—new at least for most theists—in its conception of God as a kind of modified utilitarian. This conception resulted from the need to reconcile the evident hardships and suffering present in the struggle for existence with a faith in a God both immanent and benevolent. A belief in a divine utilitarianism was a means of

---

[2]For accounts of this transcendental background and influence, see Persons, *loc. cit.,* and H. Burnell Pannill, *The Religious Faith of John Fiske* (Durham, N. C., 1957), pp. 43-53.

achieving this reconcilement. Though individuals might experience pain and destruction in the struggle for existence, the species, race or society benefited from the presence of these evils, and the implication was that God selected and was immanent in a process which provided for the greatest good for the greatest number. Evil was therefore an inevitable but negligible and transient factor if one kept in view the larger cosmic movement toward good.[3]

The particular system of ideas I have been describing—that is, one combining aspects of Spencerianism, transcendentalism and utilitarianism into an evolutionary theism—is perhaps most familiar to intellectual historians in the work of John Fiske. But there were numerous other popularizers of the philosophy, among whom the most important for my purposes is Joseph Le Conte, a professional scientist of international reputation, a long-time teacher at the University of California, and Frank Norris' instructor in zoology and geology.[4] Le Conte subscribed to the views which I have just explained, and he expressed them both in his classroom,

---

[3] A belief in divine utilitarianism was of course contrary to Huxley's contention that it was impossible to reconcile Christian ethics with the law of the survival of the fittest. As with the idea of immanence, divine utilitarianism derived from a theistic adaptation of Spencer, who was a utilitarian in both cosmic and individual morality. Spencer argued, on the one hand, that the presence of evil in the struggle for existence was fully justified by the larger good which resulted from the progress brought about by that struggle. (It was this position which led to the doctrine described by later historians as social Darwinism.) Spencer also maintained, on the other hand, that individual moral choice was intuitively utilitarian—that is, that the racial experience of man had produced an inherited moral sense (Spencer was a Lamarckian) which was fundamentally utilitarian in nature. Spencer thus ingeniously combined the two major streams of nineteenth-century ethical theory, a combination which suggests the way in which transcendental and utilitarian ideas coexist without clashing in the beliefs of the evolutionary theists, Le Conte and Norris. But I have simplified a complex subject, since evolutionary theists also tended to avoid some of the harsher implications of cosmic utilitarianism by attributing to man the unique ability to progress by the practice of love (that is, through cooperation rather than conflict) as he evolved toward complete expression of the divine spirit within him. For example, the position of such an evolutionary theist as John Fiske (see his *The Idea of God* [Boston, 1885], p. 163) was that though strife was still a current mode of progress, "a stage of civilization will be reached in which human sympathy shall be all in all, and the spirit of Christ shall reign supreme throughout the length and breadth of the earth."

[4] I discuss at length Le Conte's philosophical ideas, and Norris' knowledge and acceptance of them, in my "Evolutionary Ethical Dualism in Frank Norris' *Vandover and the Brute* and *McTeague*," *PMLA*, LXXVI (December, 1961), 552-60. For other discussions of Le Conte, see Persons, *loc. cit.*, and Eugene W. Hilgard, "Biographical Memoir of Joseph Le Conte," in *Biographical Memoirs of the National Academy of Sciences*, VI (1909), pp. 147-218.

as he tells us in his autobiography,[5] and in his major philosophical work, *Evolution: Its Nature, Its Evidences, and Its Relation to Religious Thought,* first published in 1888. Carefully attempting to distinguish between pantheism and immanence, he rested his evolutionary theism upon the premise that "God may be conceived as self-sundering his Energy, and setting over against himself a part as Nature."[6] To Le Conte, therefore,

> God is immanent, resident in Nature. Nature is the house of many mansions in which he dwells. The forces of Nature are different forms of his energy acting directly at all times and in all places. The laws of nature are modes of operation of the omnipresent Divine energy, invariable because he is perfect. The objects of Nature are objectified, externalized—materialized states of Divine consciousness, or Divine thoughts objectified by the Divine will.[7]

All nature to Le Conte is thus both natural—that is, available to scientific observation and describable by scientific laws—and supernatural, for "all is permeated with the immediate Divine presence."[8] Like Fiske, then, Le Conte believed that the road for man's salvation lay *Through Nature to God.*[9]

Now the primary question is how this system of belief operates in *The Octopus.*[10] I do not want to suggest that Norris was a student of contemporary philosophy. I believe, however, that he sufficiently understood and accepted the basic premises of evolutionary theism to recognize their applicability in a novel centering

---

[5]*The Autobiography of Joseph Le Conte,* ed. William D. Armes (New York, 1903), p. 257.

[6]Quoted from Le Conte's comments on Josiah Royce's *The Conception of God: An Address Before the Union* (Berkeley, 1895). Le Conte, in this brief reply to Royce's address, sums up the basic position of his *Evolution.*

[7]*Evolution* ... (2d ed., rev.; New York, 1891), p. 353.

[8]*Ibid.,* p. 356. I omit in this brief summary of Le Conte's evolutionary theism two of his major ideas—that of evolutionary stages and that of ethical dualism —both of which are more important for Norris' early work than for the epic of the wheat novels.

[9]John Fiske, *Through Nature to God* (Boston, 1899).

[10]Although Franklin Walker pointed out in 1932 the possible influence of Le Conte on Norris, Robert D. Lundy is the only critic to discuss *The Octopus* in connection with Le Conte's ideas. See Walker, *Frank Norris: A Biography* (Garden City, N. Y., 1932), pp. 58, 75 and Lundy, "The Making of *McTeague* and *The Octopus*" (Doctor's thesis, University of California, 1956). Mr. Lundy's basic intent is to suggest that Le Conte's evolutionary optimism is the source of the artistic flaws in *The Octopus;* my purpose is to trace the unified system of ideas operative in the novel.

on man's relationship to nature. He probably absorbed these premises from Le Conte during his Berkeley years, and then found confirmation or revitalization of them in the ideas of William Rainsford, a Christian evolutionist clergyman whom he knew in New York.[11] But whatever their source, the three aspects of evolutionary theism which I have sketched—immanence, transcendentalism and utilitarianism—function as a cohesive and unified system in the novel.

The structural and thematic center of *The Octopus* is the growth of a crop of wheat. This cycle of growth, from October to July, contains two large substructures of conflict, both of which are resolved within the forward thrust of the wheat's growth. The first substructure deals with three young men—the poet Presley, the ascetic shepherd Vanamee and the rancher Annixter—each of whom undergoes a transformation in values and belief following a perception of the meaning of the process of growth.[12] The second substructure is that of the struggle for the wheat by the ranchers and the railroad, each seeking the largest possible profit from its growth. Let me discuss these substructures individually in order to indicate how each contributes to an evolutionary theistic conception of nature and of man's relationship to nature.

First, however, it is important to recognize that Norris establishes the cycle of the wheat's growth as an epitome of the divine energy or force present in all nature and in all natural processes. As Presley views the harvested fields toward the end of the novel, he "seemed for one instant to touch the explanation of existence." The explanation is that "FORCE only existed—FORCE that brought men into the world, FORCE that crowded them out of it to make way for the succeeding generation, FORCE that made the wheat grow, FORCE that garnered it from the soil to give place to the succeeding crop."[13] This universal force inherent in

---

[11]For Rainsford and Norris, see Walker, *Frank Norris*, p. 256 and W. S. Rainsford, "Frank Norris," *World's Work*, V (April, 1903), 3276. Rainsford's *The Reasonableness of Faith and Other Addresses* (New York, 1902) reveals his Christian evolutionism.

[12]My earlier article, "Another Look at *The Octopus*," *Nineteenth-Century Fiction*, X (December, 1955), 217-24, deals with this aspect of the novel. My concern at that time, however, was almost exclusively with the process by which this transformation is achieved, rather than with the kind of knowledge dervied or the larger system of ideas in the novel.

[13]*Complete Edition of Frank Norris* (Garden City, N.Y.: Doubleday, Doran & Co., 1928), II, 343.

the life processes of both human and nonhuman existence is finally characterized by Presley as "primordial energy flung out from the hand of the Lord God himself, immortal, calm, infinitely strong."[14]

Since the wheat and its cycle of growth are made objectifications of the divine, it is not surprising that two of the central characters experience what are basically religious conversions in the presence of the wheat, and that they find confirmation for their transcendentally derived truths in the cycle of the wheat's growth. Both Annixter and Vanamee are initially isolated, troubled, fundamentally selfish men—the first dominated by fear of love, the second by hate of death. In parallel scenes each plumbs his soul in the presence of the just-emerging wheat and each struggles through to a basic truth of existence—that love is a universal benevolent force perpetually renewing life, that death of the individual is inconsequential in comparison with the continuity of life on earth. The two experiences—one centering on love, the other on death—sum up the meaning of the eternal cycle of reproduction, growth and death which man shares with all nature. On the basis of his new understanding of love. Annixter undertakes marriage in a spirit of kindness and generosity, whereas Vanamee, now accepting the transcience of death, casts aside his all-absorbing grief and embraces life. Both are now whole men who have learned that the good life is one which transcends the narrowly selfish, and both can now participate in and contribute to life. Both, in other words, have seen God in nature, rather than in Bible, church or sermon, and have reaffirmed the reality of great religious truths, though they have discovered that these truths are in actuality the eternal natural processes of life. This shaping of the supernatural into the natural is particularly clear in the case of Vanamee, who explicitly rejects the promise that his dead Angèle will be spiritally reborn. With the appearance of Angèle's daughter, however, he at last recognizes the great truth that life is eternal, whether its continuity be expressed in a new crop of wheat or in a child. At the very moment of his perception of both the new crop and the daughter, he cries out the words of St. Paul, "Oh, Grave, where is thy victory?' "[15] His exultation, however, is evolutionary rather than Christian, for he believes that Angèle's daughter is "not the symbol, but the *proof* of immortality."[16] Thus, to state it baldly, by means of the conversions of Annixter and Vanamee, Norris

---

[14]*Ibid.*
[15]*Ibid.*, p. 107.
[16]*Ibid.*, p. 106.

translates Christian love into propagation of the species, spiritual rebirth into persistence of the type. Finally, Norris presents the experiences I have been describing as moments of transcendental insight. They occur as religious experiences in which the individual imaginatively and emotionally plumbs his own soul and the natural world for the divine truths available there.

Presley, the third central character in the novel, also draws knowledge from the cycle of the wheat, but his perception is perhaps best taken up in connection with the second of the two large substructures I have indicated, that of the struggle for the wheat by the ranches and the railroad. It should be clear, however, that the vital thematic conflict within this portion of the novel is not between the ranchers and the railroad, but rather between the natural law of supply and demand and those attempting to impede or excessively exploit that law for their own interests. This larger and more inclusive conflict is more obvious in *The Pit*, where the bulls and bears are similar, despite their superficial antagonism, in their use of the need to distribute wheat as a means of speculative gain.[17] In *The Octopus* both the ranchers and the railroad greedily exploit the demand for wheat, the first by speculative "bonanza" farming, the second by monopoly of transportation. Both, moreover, engage in corrupt acts in their struggle for possession of the profitable land and its crop. There is no doubt, of course, that

---

[17]*The Pit* also contains a more extensive and simplified discussion of the omnipotence of the law of supply and demand in determining the production of wheat, an idea dramatized in *The Octopus* but introduced explicitly only briefly by Shelgrim. These few remarks of Shelgrim's, all of which derive from his idea that " 'Where there is a demand sooner or later there will be a supply' " (II, 285), have caused much auguish among readers of the novel, since Presley appears to be wholly convinced by Shelgrim's defense of the railroad as but " 'a force born out of certain conditions.' " What such readers fail to recognize is that within the context of the novel Shelgrim's use of the law of supply and demand as a defense of the railroad's practices is contravened in two major ways. First, the punishment of Behrman suggests that men are responsible for evil acts committed while participating in the fulfillment of natural laws. Secondly, Cedarquist's call for an aroused public to curb the excesses of the trust implies that such acts can be controlled to permit natural laws to operate more efficiently and with greater benefit. Norris, in other words, attributes to the railroad a conventional defense of its malpractices in order to demonstrate the falsity of that defense. Although Norris would accept Shelgrim's argument that the railroad and the farmers are inevitable forces which have risen to play necessary roles in the functioning of the law of supply and demand, he would deny Shelgrim's plea that individual railroads and individual farmers are not responsible for the ways in which they perform their roles. Presley is taken in by Shelgrim's defense because he has an incomplete awareness at this point of the relationship of individuals to natural law.

Norris considered the railroad trust the more culpable, and that he indirectly suggested means of alleviating its hold upon the community. But Norris' primary emphasis in his presentation of the struggle is that the cycle of growth and the fulfillment of demand by supply are completed regardless of whatever harm and destruction men bring upon themselves in their attempts to hinder or manipulate these natural processes for their own profit.

It is Presley who grasps the significance of the struggle for the wheat when at last that conflict is over and the crop is on its way to relieve a famine. Presley recalls the evil, pain and destruction which so disturbed him during the course of the struggle. But he now also realizes that the wheat survives as a benevolent nourisher of men. "The individual suffers," he concludes, "but the race goes on. Annixter dies, but in a far-distant corner of the world a thousand lives are saved. The larger view always and through all shams, all wickedness, discovers the Truth that will, in the end, prevail, and all things, surely, inevitably, resistlessly work together for good."[18] Presley has reached this conclusion by reminding himself of Vanamee's earlier question: "What was the larger view, what contributed the greatest good to the greatest numbers?"[19] In other words, Presley at last realizes that though individual evil and its consequences exist within the functioning of the natural law of supply and demand, that law is ultimately benefiicial for the mass of men. The famine-relieving crop of wheat concretely proves the utilitarian morality of the law determining the production of the crop. And that law, like all natural laws, is characterized by divine immanence.

In both substructures of the novel, then, the wheat functions as the objectification of divine force or energy, as God immanent, aprehendable, eternal, omnipotent and benevolent, whether that force is expressed in the wheat itself, or in the cycle of its growth, or in the law controlling its production. The wheat and its processes thus embody a moral norm, and, as in most religious systems, man may choose to recognize and obey the truths there embodied, or hazard neglect of or opposition to them. It is at this point that the two substructures of the novel unite. Man can derive great truths from the wheat, as do Annixter and Vanamee, and ally himself with its processes by accepting ideas of love and death which transcend the self. Or he can oppose himself to its lessons through selfishness, blindness or greed, as do the ranches and the

---

[18]*Complete Edition,* II, 361.

[19]*Ibid.,* p. 360. Vanamee poses this question on page 345.

railroad. God is good and God is omnipotent, but man must choose for himself whether to know and obey God and thereby receive God-given benefits.

The wheat as moral center of the novel is perhaps nowhere more apparent than in the scene in which it destroys S. Behrman. This incident is justly criticized for its melodrama; yet its melodrama is the key to its significance, since the explicit presentation of divine vengeance is almost inevitably melodramatic. For the last time Norris gives the supernatural concrete objectification, as the heavenly admonition that "vengeance is mine" is in Behrman's death obeyed to the letter. Behrman has escaped chastisement at the hands of men, and is left for the wheat. Like the evolutionary theists, then, Norris affirms the reality and immediacy of the moral order immanent in nature. Like them, he depicts this order as both natural and supernatural, though he tends to go beyond them in his eagerness to demonstrate dramatically that traditional religious beliefs are functionally operative in the processes of nature, rather than promised now and redeemable hereafter.

The flaws in the intellectual core of *The Octopus* are therefore not those of the relationship of parts to the whole. The novel makes sense within an evolutionary theistic context. Its flaws are instead of two other kinds—those arising from elements of the naïve and the ludicrous when the conventionally supernatural is translated literally into the natural, and those emerging out of the traditional paradoxes of religious faith. The latter have troubled critics the most, though commentators have usually been unaware that their primary quarrel was with such basic Christian paradoxes as the coexistence of free will and determinism, the eternity of life despite death and the emergence of good out of evil.

If these paradoxes, however, are viewed as the thematic core of *The Octopus*, they illumine the novel in two related ways. First, they indicate that its themes are above all centered in the late nineteenth-century American attempt to use new truths to confirm old ones. Secondly, they help explain the basis for the power and depth which most readers have sensed in the novel. For Norris' participation in the effort to revitalize the traditional paradoxes of religious faith invests the novel with the excitement of his desire to make intellectually and emotionally viable a deeply felt need shared by many men. In this instance, that need was to discover and to reaffirm the bases of moral order and religious faith in new worlds of experience and ideas created by a changing society and an advancing science.

Warren French

From *Frank Norris*

The traditional interpretation of *The Octopus* (1901) is summarized in the description of the novel in *The Oxford Companion to American Literature* as "dealing with the raising of wheat in California, and the struggle of the ranchers against the railroads." Coming as it did when the abusive practices of the railroads and the agitation of the enraged farmers were about to lead to major reform legislation, *The Octopus* has often been identified as either a result of the powerful Populist movement of the 1890's or a foreshadowing of the muckraking books of the early twentieth century —a kind of companion piece of Upton Sinclair's *The Jungle*.[1]

Although Norris in 1899 wrote to a Mrs. Parks that he was firmly "enlisted upon the other side" from the railroad trust and did not consider the Southern Pacific "legitimate or tolerable,"[2] there is no evidence that he was actively interested in the Populist

---

*Reprinted from *Frank Norris* (New York: Twayne Publishers, Inc., 1962), 89-106, by permission of Twayne Publishers, Inc.

[1]This interpretation is fostered by an abridgement like that in Blair, Hornberger, and Stewart's *The Literature of the United States*, revised edition, II, 618-39, which reproduces only those passages dealing with the struggle between the ranchers and the railroad.

[2]Walker, *The Letters of Frank Norris*, p. 41. He invites her to present her side.

114

movement. The only specific political reference in the novel is a derogatory mention of Lyman Derrick as the candidate of the "regular Republican" party (II, 358), and in both *The Octopus* and *A Man's Woman*, Norris offers encomia to enterprising, dynamic San Francisco businessmen. There is little evidence of any very liberal political leanings on the part of a writer who allows a sympathetically presented manufacturer to say of himself and an editor, "I don't think his editorial columns are for sale, and he doesn't believe there are blow-holes in my steel plates . . . also it appears that we have more money than Henry George believes to be right" (*A Man's Woman*, VI, 231). Ernest Marchand wondered why Norris had suddenly become interested in sociological questions when he came to write *The Octopus*, for "not a whisper" of such occurrences as the Homestead and Pullman strikes are heard in his earlier books. The answer very probably is that Norris was not so much interested in specific problems as in finding illustrations for his general theories of the proper conduct of life. We shall see that he does not really sympathize with either side in the struggle he depicts in *The Octopus*. He appears to have embraced Populist causes only when these chanced to coincide with his preconceived notions; and, although Norris was associated with *McClure's*, one of the magazines most closely connected with the muckracking movement, he left its employ and New York without regret before the movement had gotten up full steam.

As early as the socially conscious 1930's in fact, reform-minded critics began to doubt if *The Octopus* was even the work of the socially enlightened determinist that Norris was sometimes reputed to be. Granville Hicks pointed out in *The Great Tradition* that it was impossible to reconcile a strict determinism with a faith in all things working inevitably toward the good, and others were quick to seize his point and to charge Norris with being "confused." That critics might have been confused and Norris perfectly consistent but misunderstood seems not to have occurred to anyone until the vogue for social reform literature had begun to wane with the passing of the worst of the Depression.

The road to a greater understanding of Norris' "lost frontier" epic was paved in 1940 by "Norris Explains *The Octopus*," an article in which H. Willard Reninger compares the novelist's critical theories with his practice. Citing the shepherd Vanamee's important conversation with the poet Presley near the end of the novel, Reninger points out that the whole work demonstrates the viewpoint Vanamee enunciates when he tells his listener that if he looks at disaster "from the vast height of humanity . . . you will find, if our view be large enough, that it is *not* evil, but good, that in the end remains" (II,345). Thus Reninger explains that the "alleged inconsistencies" in the novel are reconciled by an all-encompassing philosophy:

> The novel dramatizes the doctrine that although men in a given locality can be temporarily defeated by combined economic and political forces, which in themselves are temporary and contigent on a phase of civilization, the *natural forces,* epitomized by the wheat, which are eternal and resistless, will eventually bring about the greatest good for the greatest number.[3]

Reninger's analysis is helpful, but not sufficiently critical of Norris' failure to carry out his theories. Reninger cites the novelist's demand that artists probe deeply into the motives of those "type men" who stand for the multitude, but he does not observe that Norris understood little about underlying human motives and that he usually brushes aside hard-to-analyze behavior as instinctive. Reninger takes Norris' ideas too much at their author's declared value; and since he dismisses Vanamee's mysticism as "merely a technique" Norris used, he fails not only to ask why only the shepherd is triumphant in his quest but also whether Norris was really conscious of all the ideas that influenced his interpretation of the events he employed.

Weaknesses of previous interpretations of the novel, including Reninger's, are well demonstrated in George Meyer's "New Interpretation" (*College English,* March, 1943). Meyer is the first to point out that Norris' opinion of the ranchers in the novel has been misconstrued and that he saw them not as "poor folks"— like the migrants in *The Grapes of Wrath* or victims of the system like the workers in *The Jungle*—but as "reckless would-be profiteers, as speculators so unfortunate as to be less powerful and ingenious than their competitors in a ruinous struggle for economic power."

He also corrects a long-standing misapprehension of the book by identifying Shelgrim, the railroad president who talks of nature in order "to rationalize his own irresponsibility," and not Norris as the fatalist. He also points out that the poet Presley is not a

---

[3]H. Willard Reninger, "Norris Explains *The Octopus:* A Correlation of His Theory and Practice," *American Literature,* XII, 225 (May, 1940).

self-portrait of the author and that the tragedy depicted here need not invariably be repeated, because the reader can learn from the misfortunes of others. He recognizes, too, that the novel is a kind of transcendentalist tract illustrating Norris' "conviction that Americans wrought unnecessary evil by supporting an economic system that clashed violently with the facts of nature," the principal one of which is that "the wheat will flow irresistibly from the field where it is grown to mouths that need to be fed" and that the natural force of the movement "injures or destroys many individuals unlucky enough to be standing in its path."

Meyer's article might have provided a definitive reading of the novel if he had not considerably overestimated the author's capacity for abstract thinking. When he insists that Norris thought that, if men would cooperate with one another, they might eliminate the disastrous role that chance plays in human affairs, he fails to see the significance of the Vanamee subplot (he treats the shepherd only as a mouthpiece for certain views), and he ignores Norris' frequently reiterated preference for *doing* over *thinking*, since cooperation with other men (although not with the "forces of nature") requires even more thought than action.

A careful, thorough, rational scholar himself, writing during a period of grave international crisis, Meyer fails to give sufficient emphasis to the mystical elements in Norris' thought, his preoccupation with "sixth senses," and his disdain for liberal education. The critic tries too hard to make the novel fit the pattern of the traditional reformist tract because he does not see that Norris was as suspicious of cooperation between individual men as he was of conflict between them.

Both Reninger and Meyer are correct in perceiving that *The Octopus* is internally consistent, but neither pays sufficient attention to the extent to which irrational elements influenced Norris' thought. Only by careful examination of the Vanamee subplot is it possible to observe the extent to which Norris tried to incorporate a good example, as well as several horrible ones, into the first volume of his epic trilogy.

This subplot has not always received the attention it deserves, because in *The Octopus*—as in other works—Norris' skill as a reporter caused the depiction of specific evils that were not his essential concern to overshadow the general moral he wished to convey. Although the book has been often reprinted and summarized, we should perhaps before beginning an analysis recall the

major events of the involved plot Norris built around the notorious
Mussel Slough affair, in which the exploitative practices of the
railroads led to armed rebellion.[4]

It is not always sufficiently acknowledged that the novel is an
exercise in point of view. What it contains is what Presley, a
poet somewhat reminiscent of Edwin Markham, sees during
a summer that he spends in the San Joaquin Valley trying to discover a purpose and a direction for his own work. He is a guest
of Magnus Derrick, an ex-governor who farms one of the largest
ranches in the valley. Unfortunately Derrick—like most of his
neighbors—does not have clear title to his property. Much of it
belongs to the Pacific and Southwestern Railroad, "The Octopus,"
which has promised—but not contracted—sometime to sell the
land to the ranchers at a low price. A crisis is precipitated when,
at the height of a party, news arrives that the railroad demands
that the ranchers either pay an exorbitant price for the properties
they have improved or be evicted. When the railroad attempts to
have a Federal posse evict the ranchers, an armed battle ensues
in which six of the ranchers—including Derrick's son and his
neighbor, Annixter—are killed. Derrick is further discredited
when it is revealed that he has used bribery to buy a position on
the state railroad commission for his son Lyman, who sells out to
the railroads anyway. Like Curtis Jadwin in *The Pit*, Magnus
Derrick speculates desperately and is utterly shattered.

Others suffer as well. Dyke, a loyal employee whom the railroad
unjustly discharges and then bankrupts, turns train robber and
goes to prison. Mrs. Hooven, widow of one of the ranch-hands
killed in the skirmish, starves to death in San Francisco. Even
Behrman, the principal agent of the railroad, who seems immune
to human justice, is—in one of Norris' most spectacular scenes—
finally smothered in the hold of a ship that is being loaded with his
own wheat. Presley survives, but he leaves California, saddened by
the death of his friends and convinced that he is ineffectual as
either poet or man of action.

The only major character to survive the holocaust is Vanamee,
a shepherd who some years before the story begins had withdrawn
from society after his sweetheart was mysteriously assaulted and
died in childbirth. Living close to nature, he has developed myste-

---

[4]The historical background of this novel and of other works dealing with the
same incident is explained in Irving McKee's "Notable Memorials to Mussel
Slough," *Pacific Historical Review*, XVII, 19-27 (February, 1948).

rious telepathic powers, and he is finally rewarded for his renuncia-
tion of self-destructive ambition by winning the love of his former
sweetheart's daughter.

All of these events are usually interpreted as adding up to an
attack upon the railroad and to a paean of praise for the wheat—
the irresistible life-force that frustrates those seemingly beyond
the reach of human justice. Such an interpretation does not, however, satisfactorily explain all of the novel—especially the concluding sentiment that "in every crisis of the world's life . . . if your
view be large enough . . . it is *not* evil, but good, that in the end
remains."

A good approach to the matters needing attention is through
Donald Pizer's recent "Another Look at *The Octopus*," which
restates Meyer's interpretation of Norris' attitude toward the
ranchers as "speculators" and adds two further observations that
aid understanding of the novel. First, Pizer shows that the story
essentially concerns educating the poet Presley into a recognition
of the insignificance of the individual in comparison to the operation of the great, benevolent forces of nature. Then he points out
the novel's relationship to transcendental thought.

Basically, Pizer maintains, Norris is looking not confidently
forward but nostalgically backward, since his "faith in individual
perception of Truth and in the concomitant dependence upon a
benevolent nature in discerning this Truth found its most distinc-
tive statement in the transcendental movement."[5] Pizer argues, as
I do throughout this study, that Norris—driven by fear and distrust
of contemporary civilization—sought principally to turn back the
clock.

Ironically, Norris might have produced a more impressive
work if he had been less nostalgic. As an angry plea for the
rectification of specific evils, *The Octopus* is one of the most
powerful tracts ever penned. Those who extract the story of the
struggle between the ranchers and the railroad from the rest of
the book are to a certain extent justified by the result. Judged,
however, on the basis of what the author, and not posthumous
editors, considered essential, the work fails to convey its full
message convincingly not because of internal inconsistencies—
since the final pages advance arguments that reconcile seeming
internal contradictions—but because of the lack of examples to

---

[5]Donald Pizer, "Another Look at *The Octopus*," *Nineteenth-Century Fiction*,
X, 224 (December, 1955).

support these arguments adequately. In the long run evil may
be less enduring than good, but Norris as a journalist depicts
the short-range victory of evil more convincingly than as a
novelist he demonstrates the ultimate triumph of good.

But about the supposed inconsistencies—charges that the novel
is confused have generally centered upon two passages: Presley's
incredible interview with Shelgrim, a railroad president apparently
modeled on Collis Huntington of the Southern Pacific, and the
concluding statement that "all things, surely, inevitably, resistlessly work together for the good."

Certainly the Shelgrim episode (II, 281-86) distorts the structure of the novel and begins to make us suspect the artistic
integrity of a writer who peremptorily introduces a new viewpoint into a nearly completed work. To claim, however, as Ernest
Marchand does, that after the interview "Norris walked arm in
arm with [Presley] and shared his bewilderment" is to continue
the unjustified identification of author and his character and
to miss the real point of the incident.

During the interview, Shelgrim makes the often quoted statement, "You are dealing with forces, young man, when you speak
of Wheat and the Railroads, not with men. . . . If you want to
fasten the blame of the affair at Los Muertos on any one person,
you will make a mistake. Blame conditions, not men" (II, 285).
Presley regains the street "stupefied." He cannot refute this new
idea, which "rang with the clear reverberation of truth" and he
asks if anyone were "to blame for the horror at the irrigating
ditch" where so many of his friends died.

These doubts, however, are Presley's, not Norris'. What his
happened here—as elsewhere—is that Norris has botched the
writing. The book is easily misread not because it expresses
subtle ideas—the thinking is often quite simple-minded—but
because Norris' writing about ideas is often muddy, and it is
not easy to distinguish between what he thinks and what his
characters think. We must recall, however, that despite the furore
over his poem "The Toilers," (a work similar to Edwin Markham's
"The Man with the Hoe"), Presley—as shown by an unsuccessful
speech he delivers to a group of ranchers and by his abortive
bombing of the villain's house—is not effective as either thinker
or doer, as a handler of either symbols or things.

Far from identifying himself with Presley (although they share
some ideas), Norris throughout the book treats the poet with mild
contempt as a "type" illustrative of the ineffectiveness of the
literary man in coping with the violent forces in the world.

That Norris was also not taken in by the arguments he assigns Shelgrim is demonstrated later when at a society dinner he depicts Presley beginning to think things over and—in what Maxwell Geismar calls "the intellectual climax of the novel"—realizing that he has been duped by the fast-talking Shelgrim:

> The railroad might indeed be a force only, which no man could control and for which no man was responsible, but his friends had been killed, but years of extortion and oppression had wrung money from all of the San Joaquin, money that had made possible this very scene in which he found himself. . . . It was a half-ludicrous, half-horrible "dog eat dog," an unspeakable cannibalism (II, 317).

Presley foresees that some day the people will rise and in turn "rend those who now preyed upon them." As George Meyer points out, Shelgrim uses "natural forces" as a rationalization for his own irresponsibility. Despite his high position, the railroad president is simply a confidence man, one who overwhelms counter-argument by a skillful use of question-begging and of faulty dilemmas (irresponsible operation or bankruptcy.)

Norris puts his finger on the real trouble when he says that "No standards of measure in [Presley's] mental equipment would apply to [Shelgrim] . . . not because these standards were different in kind, but that they were lamentably deficient in size" (II, 284). The forces at work are not necessarily uncontrollable (Marchand points out that "the growing of wheat is not a cosmic process, but a purely human activity"), but they cannot be controlled by the characters Norris has created.

To dwell on the insufficiency of his characters' mental equipment, however, would defeat the author's purpose, for it would conflict with the uncritical enthusiasm he expresses elsewhere when he asks about his "sturdy American" actors: "Where else in the world round were such strong, honest men, such strong, beautiful women?" (II, 217). The question is intended to be rhetorical; but it might be answered, "Anywhere that people are strong-minded enough to control the forces civilization has created." Norris has not proved that these forces cannot be controlled, but only that he cannot conceive the characters who could control them. He then proceeds to display unfounded confidence in himself by assuming that he knows as much about human capability as anyone.

This unwarranted confidence is responsible for what many readers consider the dogmatism of the conclusion. How did Norris know that "all things surely, inevitably, resistlessly work together for the good"? Why, he just knew it, and the reader who will not take his word for it is obviously as much out of harmony with the secret forces of nature as the ill-fated ranchers of the San Joaquin Valley. Part of the strength of Norris' work is that he never felt any doubt about his own perspicacity.

Probably more as model or "type" than proof of his theories, Norris did weave into his epic tale of the fall of the foolish, the tale of Vanamee as a kind of counter-narrative to guide those who seek the right road. This story is not usually credited with its proper importance in the over-all design of the novel, for the lonely shepherd is often ignored or mentioned only as spokesman for the philosophy that colors the final pages of the book. Yet even if Norris had not especially spoken in a letter to Isaac Marcosson of this subplot as "even mysticism . . . a sort of allegory,"[6] the amount of space he lavished upon the story and the fact that it is Vanamee's philosophy that is repeated at the end of the book should alert readers to the significance of the only major character in the story who emerges triumphant.

The shepherd enunciates the philosophy that "in every crisis of the world's life . . . if your view be large enough . . . it is *not* evil, but good, that in the end remains." We need not, however, take his word for this; his own story is supposed to illustrate the truth of the premise just as much as the story of the ranchers and their struggle against the railroad is supposed to illustrate the truth of the premise that those who stand in the way of irresistible forces will be destroyed.

Vanamee is a kind of latter-day Thoreau, "a college graduate and a man of wide reading and great intelligence, [who] had chosen to lead his own life, which was that of a recluse" (I, 33). Unlike Thoreau, however, his withdrawal from society is not an experiment, but a permanent policy. In view of the final contrast between what happens to him and to the others in the novel, we must conclude that Norris thought that the sensitive, introspective person could regain harmony with nature only by completely rejecting civilized society.

Vanamee loved Angèle Varian, who lived on a flower ranch near the mission where he met her nightly. One night, however, Angèle was met by a never identified "other," who raped her. When she died in childbirth, "the thread of Vanamee's life had been snapped" (I, 37).

---

[6]Walker (ed.), *The Letters of Frank Norris,* p. 67.

As a result of his long isolation from society, Vanamee has developed a strange power to call other people to him. ("If I had wanted to, sir, I could have made you come to me from back there in the Quien Sabe ranch," he tells a priest.) He does not understand this power himself ("I understand as little of these things as you," he tells the priest, when asked about the power [I, 133]). Finally after eighteen years he returns to the scene of Angèle's rape and begins calling for her, demanding that God answer with "something real, even if the reality were fancied" (I, 145). Through a succession of scenes, we see the answer to this totally irrational call gradually materialize until at last "Angèle was realized in the Wheat" (II, 347).

The "answer" is Angèle's daughter, who has come in response to Vanamee's mysterious calls and who even more mysteriously loves him as her mother did. Her coming demonstrates specifically how good—in the large enough view—comes out of evil. The rape and death of Angèle were evil, but the child born of this bestiality is good. Norris even has Vanamee make this point specifically: "I believed Angèle dead. I wept over her grave; mourned for her as dead in corruption. She has come back to me, more beautiful than ever" (II, 345).

Does this example prove the sweeping generalization Norris makes at the end of the book? Probably many citics have overlooked the whole business because few could concede that it did. Even if we were willing to grant that one example might be enough to support a theory about the operation of the Universe, we could not overlook the extraordinary aspects of the particular situation—Vanamee's mysterious ability to use a kind of telepathic hypnosis (he speaks of a "sixth sense" or "a whole system of other unnamed senses" experienced by "people who live alone and close to nature"), and Angèle's daughter's remarkable duplication of not only her mother's appearance, but also her feelings.

What is Norris trying to say here? We cannot, of course, disprove telepathy, "sixth senses," and the transmigration of souls that he seems to be hinting at any more than he can prove their existence with this wild romance that most critics of the book have apparently found too embarrassing to discuss. But what we can say is that it is hard to imagine what Norris does mean if not that we must either put up with injustice and abuse, temporary "evils" of civilization, or else reject civilization altogether and take to the woods where we can develop "unnamed senses." If man's problem is to improve conditions in the world he has made, Norris is no help. He is rather like the man who, unable to do something himself, announces that it cannot be done and sits scoffing at those who try. Although he lived in a society full of worshippers of progress, with whom he is sometimes confused, he himself is a self-appointed propagandist for "hard" primitivism.

Another indication of the backwardness of Norris' thought is the really most remarkable part of the interview with Shelgrim, the railroad president—not the blatant sophistries about "forces," but the vignette of Shelgrim granting another chance to a drunken bookkeeper, an act that shatters Presley's concept of the executive as a bloodsucker. The reader may well ask along with Presley how the man who can handle an erring underling so intelligently and humanely can have treated so inhumanely the ranchers and Dyke, a once faithful employee whom the agents of the "octopus" drive to robbery, murder, and death.

The answer is that Shelgrim, as Norris conceives of him, is not really a competent administrator of a vast business, even though Norris may have drawn the incident from his own knowledge of the railroad executives. Actually the behavior that it illustrates can best be analyzed in the light of a passage from Steinbeck's *The Grapes of Wrath*, in which a dispossessed tenant ponders:

> "Funny thing, how it is. If a man owns a little property, that property is him, it's part of him, and it's like him. . . . Even if he isn't successful, he's big with property. . . . But let a man get property that he doesn't see, or can't take time to get his fingers in, or can't be there to walk on it—why, then the property is the man. He can't do what he wants, he can't think what he wants. The property is the man, stronger than he is. And he is small, not big. Only his possessions are big—and he's the servant of his property."[7]

This is a classic statement of the view of the "thing-handler" as opposed to the "symbol-handler"—that man can understand only that which he can actually see and feel. The tenant has grounds for his observation, because many men who have actually only the education and intelligence to be "thing-handlers" have been forced into or have taken upon themselves the roles of "symbol-handlers," with the distressing result that conditions

---

[7]*The Grapes of Wrath* (New York, 1939), pp. 50-51. In this chapter, Steinbeck attributes to the bankers and their agents who are dispossessing the sharecropers, the same rationalizations Shelgrim uses to exonerate himself.

occur like those depicted in both *The Octopus* and *The Grapes of Wrath*.

Actually Norris foreshadows part of Steinbeck's tenant's speech in his analysis of Magnus Derrick, the elder statesman among the ranchers:

> It was the true California spirit that found expression through him, the spirit of the West, unwilling to occupy itself with details, unwilling to wait, to be patient, to achieve by legitimate plodding. . . . It was in this frame of mind that Magnus and the multitude of other ranchers of whom he was a type, farmed their ranches. *They had no love for their land.* They were not attached to their soil. . . . To get all there was out of the land, to squeeze it dry, to exhaust it, seemed their policy. When, at last, the land worn out, would refuse to yield, they would invest their money in something else; by then, they would all have made their fortunes. They did not care. "After us the deluge" (II, 14; italics mine).

The charge here is the same as that against the bankers in *The Grapes of Wrath*, and those who have supposed that Norris was as critical of the ranchers as of the railroads have been right as far as they have gone; but they should have gone further. He is actually more critical of the ranchers, because the point of the incident of Shelgrim's kindness is to suggest that he does actually love those around him—those with whose problems he is personally acquainted.

What Norris failed to see is that man of such limited vision would be incompetent to operate successfully a vast railroad or any comparable enterprise since he would be unable to do what competent administrators of vast affairs must do if they are not to court disaster—set up and administer equitably and impartially uniform regulations for those with whom they deal directly and those with whom they do not. Of course such competent administrators were uncommon in the nineteenth century (they are still not especially abundant), but commercial disasters were fairly common. Many businesses and institutions (including the railroads) are still paying for the incompetence of the "self-made" administrators of the Gilded Age. Norris' shortcoming was that he reported ably enough what he saw, but he failed to perceive what was wrong. He stepped into the trap that awaits many uncritical admirers of the empire builder—the assumption that those who have the force and energy to put together an empire

necessarily have the intelligence and patience to administer it
adequately. A reporter, of course, would not be handicapped by
making such an erroneous assumption, but it is likely to prove
crippling to a man seeking to formulate rules for the conduct
of life.

Ernest Marchand is right when he says that the real struggle
in *The Octopus* is between "two types of economy"—the old,
vanishing agricultural, and the rising industrial; but he does not
see that both economies are administered in this novel by the
same type of chieftain, since the author had no concept that a
more complicated economy demands a new, more thoughtful type
of leadership.

Norris got close enough to the ranchers to see their weaknesses,
but he did not get as close to the managers of the railroad. *The
Octopus* has often been called one-sided, but it has not been
pointed out that the result of the oversimplified treatment of the
railroad's role in the controversy is that it actually comes off better
than it might because Norris was too busy looking for evil to notice
incompetence. Shelgrim easily rationalizes away charges of mal-
feasance by blaming evils on forces rather than men, but he could
not so easily dispose of charges of misfeasance or non-feasance.

Norris' naïveté in the presence of empire builders recalls that
the one striking exception to his attack upon civilization is his
praise in *A Man's Woman* and "The Frontier Gone at Last" of
those conquerors of the physical frontier who are now tackling
the economic frontier. In "The True Reward of the Novelist,"
he had also observed that the "financier and poet" are alike, "so
only they be big enough" (VII, 17). He was probably dazzled
enough by Huntington, who supported the *Wave*, to suppose him
a truly great and good financier, just as he probably supposed
himself a great and good artist.

An illustration of his susceptibility to the word-magic of the
business titan occurs in *The Octopus* when Cedarquist, a prom-
inent industrialist, after denouncing San Francisco's failure to
support *his* iron works, which he calls an "indifference to *public*
affairs" (my italics and shades of Charlie Wilson!), goes on:

> "The great word of the nineteenth century has been Production.
> The great word of the twentieth century will be—listen to me,
> you youngsters—Markets. As a market for our Production . . . our
> *Wheat*, Europe is played out. . . . We supply more than Europe can
> eat, and down go the prices. The remedy is *not* in the curtailing of

our wheat areas, but in this, we must have new markets, greater markets. . . . We must march with the course of empire, not against it. I mean, we must look to China (II, 21-22).

What Cedarquist advocates is not spreading civilization, but simply disseminating stuff—things not ideas. He simply seeks to exert some mysterious power over others, and he is no more willing than Vanamee to accept responsibility for it. His talk of "marching with the course of empire" simply advocates doing rather than thinking—action for its own sake, like the irresistible action of unthinking nature.

From this passage we can see how Norris can speak of nature at times as indifferent and yet at others as good. By *indifferent*, he does not mean what a non-teleological thinker would. He probably could not even conceive of the universe without "a sense of obligation" that Stephen Crane personifies in a poem. *Indifferent* to him simply means *unconscious*. Nature, he feels, does good without thinking about it—but it does do good in the long run. Indeed his opinion is that most of the trouble begins when people start thinking instead of feeling. Without thought, of course, one can have no sense of responsibility; but this did not disturb Norris, for he assumed that one who acted according to the proper "natural" feelings could do no wrong and would not need to worry about consequences.

We should not be surprised, however, that Norris does not insist that his characters be responsible for their actions, since he is irresponsible himself. His lack of responsibility, in fact, accounts for some of the most striking features of *The Octopus*. An example is a section of the novel which some critics have praised in which glimpses of Mrs. Hooven starving to death outside are alternated with glimpses of the guests of a railroad magnate gorging themselves on fancy food inside (II, 302-22). Actually this is one of the most meretricious pieces of writing in the novel since it directly contradicts Norris' principle of writing about representative situations in order to lead to general statements about the operation of the universe. Here he uses a most extraordinary coincidence to agitate the reader's feelings. The point is not that readers should not be moved by Mrs. Hooven's sufferings and infuriated that they can occur in such a place, but that— if Norris' main point that everything works inevitably for the good is true—the sensations provoked by this incident are gratuitous. Such material has a place in the novel of social protest, but here

Norris appears merely to be exploiting misery in order to display his talent. He is obliging the reader to indulge in the worst kind of sentimentality—to revel in feeling for its own sake, a kind of emotional masturbation. It is not surprising that the man capable of producing this passage completely failed to understand Harriet Beecher Stowe's motives in writing *Uncle Tom's Cabin*.

Another big scene—that in which S. Behrman, the agent of the railroad whose principle is "all that the traffic will bear," suffocates in the hold of a wheat ship—is suspect for different reasons. Coming near the end of the novel, the scene at first appears a masterpiece of ironic symbolism: Behrman, seemingly impervious to any attack by man, is overwhelmed at last by the irresistible force of the wheat he had hoped to exploit. The fat, rich man is killed by the very substance that promises life to starving Asiatics. The scene very well demonstrates Norris' doctrine that men, "motes in the sunshine," might perish while the WHEAT remains (II, 360; capitals Norris').

Yet once again in creating this scene, Norris was gambling—quite successfully—that the reader would respond uncritically, unthinkingly. Behrman had been depicted in such a way that the reader would wish to see him punished for his offenses and would view the suffocation as a punishment—the wheat operating not as an indifferent force, but as a *deus ex machina*. To see what is wrong with the scene we need to remember that the incident could have happened to anyone; there is nothing earlier in the novel nor in the scene itself that justifies interpreting Behrman's death as retribution, except our own feelings.

As Charles Walcutt points out in *American Literary Naturalism*, Behrman is an unsatisfactory character anyway, since "his actions could be explained only by a deep-seated hatred which he is not shown to harbor." In medieval literature, he would be a stock figure—Mephistopheles, a manifestation of complete evil, immune to human attack; but in "naturalistic" fiction, he is incredible unless the work is intended primarily as a morality play.

Perhaps, however, Norris was being truly naturalistic and emphasizing the irony of the coincidence that Berhman, invulnerable to other men, was killed during a moment of triumph by natural forces beyond his control. Why then have the wheat—which in this book has been endowed with a special symbolic significance as a *creative* force—do the dirty work? It would be far more naturalistically ironic to have this self-controlled, scheming man inconspicuously killed in a situation he had no part in creating—by a bullet intended for another or a falling object. Actually Norris is trying to provide further evidence that things work inevitably, irresistibly for the good by having benevolent natural forces dispose of Behrman, but he forces his point. Sending the forces of nature to do a man's specific job both overly sentimentalizes nature and excuses man's irresponsibility—including the artist's when he falls back on gothic machinery to dispose of behavioral problems he has raised.

Earlier in this chapter, I questioned Norris' artistic integrity. The scenes I have just discussed are further evidence that defending this book against its earlier critics does not vindicate it but simply brings to light more serious flaws. But lest it appear that my only aim is to "debunk" *The Octopus*, I must make it clear that the novel is a magnificent imaginative achievement, one of the few American novels to bring a significant episode from our history to life in such a way that the reader feels he is participating in the ponderous events. Like *McTeague*, *The Octopus* compensates for its defects with vivid reporting. When we strip away the naïve arguments and the blatant attempts to titillate the reader's sentiment, we uncover a remarkable panorama of the life of a confused society torn between its desires, on the one hand, to return to the irresponsible, formless life of the frontier and, on the other, to move on to a state that might be more stable but also more chafing because one's rights and responsibilities would be spelled out by regulations.

Norris was consciously trying to produce an epic. He called his work "The epic of the Wheat," and he twice insists on comparisons with Homer (I, 42; II, 216). Despite his avowed lack of interest in style, he experimented with epic devices in this novel. The long scene in Annixter's barn was obviously influenced by the description of revels in the Homeric poems, and it even pretends to poetry through the use of refrains ("Two quarts 'n' a half. Two quarts 'n' a half." "Garnett of the Ruby Rancho, Keast from the ranch of the same name"), and they are justified only as they tie together the whirl of scenes composing this long, climactic chapter.

In a great measure, Norris himself wrote the work that he demands in "A Neglected Epic," the tale of the conquest of the West that would "devolve upon some great national event" and depict a hero who "died in defense of an ideal, an epic hero, a legendary figure, formidable, sad," who "died facing down injustice, dishonesty, and crime; died 'in his boots' " (VII, 49). Annixter meets the requirements—the clumsy misogynist who learns to love first his own wife, then "others," until his love expands to embrace the whole world on the very day that he rides to his death in defense of his homestead.

Curiously, most epics appear not at the zenith of the societies they celebrate, but in their dying days. Milton definitively stated a theology that was just losing its grip on the minds and hearts of men; Dante gave final form to the neat pigeonholes of medieval cosmology just as this rigidly structured era was about to collapse into the Renaissance; and that even Homer wrote during the last days of the patriarchal society he depicts is suggested by the mildly satirical treatment of those gods who must earlier have been fervently worshipped. By the time a way of life has become clearly enough defined and seriously enough threatened to need defending, it has usually lost its impetus and is about to collapse from physical, intellectual or moral defects.

The Octopus is the epic of the conquest of the frontier by powerful, undisciplined forces. *Doing* rather than *thinking* was needed to overcome vast and often hostile geographical forces. But with the frontier gone, the kind of freedom it had permitted and even demanded for its conquest could only either disappear too, or turn upon itself self-destructively as it does in the battle between the rancher and the railroad here celebrated. Not long after the publication of *The Octopus*, both sides were to find that because they had failed to discipline themselves they were subjected to increasing external regulation, and "frontier psychology" was to become an anachronism after the last claims were staked. Some have speculated that *The Octopus* helped to bring about the regulation of the conditions it describes, but it is more likely that the regulation was already imminent, since, like many epics, the novel dealt with conditions that could not have persisted much longer.

Like *McTeague, The Octopus* is a valuable document because it expresses a philosophy that is not a lesson to its time, but a reflection of it. Norris could not achieve the detachment of a Conrad or even a Crane, because his own ideas, fears, and prejudices were too much like those of his characters. His lack of artistic integrity is not the result of hypocrisy, but of inadequate self-analysis. In his behalf it must be pleaded that he was not like the artistic prostitutes of Madison Avenue and Hollywood who cynically manipulate the public for their own temporary advantage. Rather he was like his own characters—especially Shelgrim and Magnus Derrick, the leaders of the contending parties, who were giants in their own time—whose offense was not that they deliberately did wrong but that because of adolescent self-infatuation, they failed to perceive the limitations of their own powerful gifts.

Norris did not really know how to cope with the evils of his times; he could only advise flight. Yet he enables us to see why his contemporaries could not cope with these evils. *The Octopus* is quite unintentionally a powerful tract, because the author who trusted action over thought shows us the dangers of sharing his beliefs.

James K. Folsom

Social Darwinism or Social Protest? The 'Philosophy' of *The Octopus*

I

Most critics of *The Octopus* have been disturbed by its apparently illogical ending. Although few have been so bold as to accept the statement that Norris "flinched from drawing the strong but obvious conclusion which he had certainly prepared for,"[1] most have been uneasy about the apparent *non sequitur* with which the book ends. Norris' "cosmic optimism"[2] which attempts a justification of the ways of evolution to man by denying the whole existence of the struggle which he has just detailed in two longish volumes seems, at least, to be at variance with the apparently radical social criticism of the P. and S. W. railroad which forms the framework of the novel. A recent critic has attempted to defend

Reprinted from *Modern Fiction Studies,* VIII (Winter 1962-63), 393-400, by permission of the Purdue University-Purdue Research Foundation and the author. © 1963 by Purdue Research Foundation, Lafayette, Indiana.
[1]Paul H. Bixler, "Frank Norris's Literary Reputation," *American Literature,* VI (May, 1934), 115.
[2]I borrow this phrase from Ernest Marchand's *Frank Norris, A Study* (Stanford, California, 1942), p. 231. Marchand's remarks on *The Octopus* — as, indeed, on Norris generally — are most perceptive.

Norris against the charge of philosophical inconsistency by arguing that *The Octopus* is largely a *Bildungsroman* of the artist-hero Presley, and that much criticism of the novel "results from a lack of understanding of Norris' handling of"[3] this hero. This criticism —which is echoed by Kenneth S. Lynn in his excellent Introduction to *The Octopus*[4]—serves to draw the reader's attention to a point which has been too often ignored, that the characters in the book have a legitimate function in the novel other than acting as puppets for the author's philosophical views, but goes wrong, in my opinion, in its implicit assumption that Presley's gloss on the meaning of the book must be the true one. According to this reading, if the ending of the novel cannot be happy, or logical, or consistent, it can at least be sincere. No one has suggested, to the best of my knowledge, that the conclusion of *The Octopus* might be highly ironic, that Presley might just possibly not have the slightest idea of what he is talking about. Yet this hypothesis does not seem to me to be far-fetched on the basis of a close reading of the novel.

From the beginning to the end of *The Octopus* Presley is concerned with writing the epic of the West, but is unable to arrive at a true artistic grasp of his subject. When we first meet him, significantly, we find him unable to write the epic because "all the noble poetry" of his view of the way western life ought to be "seemed in his mind to be marred and disfigured by the presence of certain immovable facts" (p. 9). He cannot see, we discover, how to combine these "immovable facts" of the ranchers' struggle with the Railroad with that "rose-coloured mist . . . that dulled all harsh outlines, all crude and violent colours" (p. 9), which is, to his mind, the proper concern of the epic. All Presley's rhetoric should not blind us to the fact that he is never able to solve this problem. At the end of the novel as at the beginning the epic of the West remains unwritten. Presley's real difficulty, however, is not so much that he is unable to combine the poetry with the facts as it is that he is unable to understand the facts or, more important, to grasp their relevance. He is given to grandiose visions which he often mistakes for grand ones. Norris takes great pains to drive the point home. Presley's first soliloquy, given as he strolls across one of the huge

---

[3] Donald Pizer, "Another Look at *The Octopus*," *Nineteenth-Century Fiction.* X (December, 1955), 217. Mr. Pizer's study gives a valuable summary of Norris's alleged philosophical inconsistencies.

[4] (Boston, 1958), pp. v-xxv. Subsequent citations to *The Octopus,* enclosed in the text, refer to this edition.

ranches to an unexpected meeting with the shepherd Vanamee, is a case in point, a very apotheosis of the general. Buck Annixter, from whose home Presley has set out, has told him that he should keep watch for a huge herd of sheep as he walks, concluding with the not completely gratuitous wise-crack that Presley "might write a poem about 'em. Lamb—ram; sheep graze—sunny days. Catch on?" (p. 21). Presley's vision, however, is not concerned with such mundane matters as sheep. Gazing from the top of a hill on the ranch, he forgets both sheep and Annixter in the magnificent view of the San Joaquin valley and even subsumes the great ranches themselves as "mere accessories, irrelevant details" to this quasi-epic vision which sets his "morbid super-sensitive mind reeling, *drunk with the intoxication of mere immensity*" (p. 33—italics mine). This preoccupation with size alone is Presley's great artistic failing. His inability to write his epic is paradoxically due to the fact that his vision is too grand, too immense, too all-encompassing. The true concern of the epic, as the capitalist Cedarquist tells him at a chance meeting in San Francisco, is the struggle of the farmer with the Trust (p. 209), a struggle which Presley has previously dismissed somewhat contemptuously as mere "living issues" which serve only to distract him from his proper subject (p. 206). Ironically, Presley's one decent poetic work, his poem "The Toilers," is inspired by those very "living issues" which he affects to despise. Norris very nicely makes the point here that "immovable facts" are in their very nature poetic rather than, as Presley supposes, essentially unartistic. Toward the end of the book Presley himself confesses that everything he has attempted, "his great epic, his efforts to help the people who surrounded him, even his attempted destruction of the enemy, all . . . had come to nothing" (p. 389). And indeed, even he has some inkling of the reason, albeit only a vague one. After the failure of his melodramatic speech at the protest meeting in Bonneville, a speech which is applauded "vociferously but perfunctorily" by an audience of ranchers who feel that it might be considered eloquent by "more educated" men, Presley realizes that he cannot really move the people because he does not understand them, that he is "an outsider to their minds" (p. 379), that he has not grasped the nature of their problems, of the "immovable facts" of life in the San Joaquin valley.

That such a man as Presley should after mature deliberation accept the theory that "the larger view always and through all shams, all wickedness, discovers the Truth that will, in the end, prevail' (p. 448) is in itself no very compelling reason that we, as readers, also adopt this position. This hypothesis seems, in fact, to appeal to the inherent weakness in Presley's character, the temptation to discover such a large view that troublesome "immovable facts" will not intrude, or at least not be noticed amidst the universal harmony. And our doubts about the inherent validity of this thesis are not immediately put at rest when we consider its author and eloquent propounder, the mystical shepherd Vanamee.

When we first meet Vanamee,[5] he has been hired to tend the immense herd of sheep which are grazing on Annixter's Quien Sabe Rancho. Presley, upon encountering him, finds him just preparing to leave his charges in order to visit Father Sarria at the Mission in Guadalajara. Vanamee blithely abandons the animals to the care of his dogs and an invisible assistant and starts off with Presley toward the Mission. Presley wonders at the "heedlessness" (p. 29) of leaving the sheep, but since Vanamee presumably knows more about sheep than he does, says nothing. The result is what Presley had suspected: the sheep wander onto the railroad right-of-way, are hit by a passing train, and a great many are killed. The abandoning of the sheep is not only a touch of sentimentality to remind us of the inhumanity of the Railroad. A few pages earlier we had been told how Vanamee had inadvertently failed to guard another innocent creature under his protection with similar results; his betrothed, Angéle, had been raped by a mysterious Other who, like the fast passenger locomotive, had appeared without warning. With fine irony Norris has made his point: appearances can be deceiving and a man with sheep is not necessarily a good shepherd.

Having left the sheep to their fate, Vanamee and Presley visit Father Sarria at the Mission. Presley, realizing the other two wish to be alone, soon makes his excuses and departs. After he has gone, Father Sarria and Vanamee turn to a discussion of the mysterious death of Angéle at the hands of the Other. Vanamee, we discover, has telepathic powers, and is going to use them to attempt to call Angéle back from the grave. Father Sarria is naturally shocked at Vanamee's idea and reminds him that the ways of God are not to bring the dead back to life. Vanamee admits the truth of this, concluding rather lamely that he feels if he "only knew how to use the strength of [his] will" he could "not call her back—but—something—." Father Sarria politely but pointedly answers that "a

---

[5]For what it is worth the name "Vanamee" itself may have symbolic overtones. Just as "Angéle, his betrothed, is in his eyes an "angel," so his own name suggests *"vain ami,"* and foreshadows the role which he plays throughout the novel, that of Job's comforter.

diseased and distorted mind is capable of hallucinations," if that is
what Vanamee means; and Vanamee, for the moment convinced,
replies, "perhaps that is what I mean. Perhaps I want only the
delusion, after all" (p. 102). When, despite Father Sarria's warning, Vanamee goes back to his telepathic quest, it comes as no
surprise to the reader that a delusion is precisely what he finds.
Norris' whole ironic point about the value of these occult re-
searches is bound up with the metaphor of the wheat, a metaphor
which, significantly, is first made explicit in this same scene. Father
Sarria, in attempting to comfort Vanamee for the loss of Angéle,
mentions St. Paul's parable of the grain of wheat which is "not
quickened except it die' and "is sown a natural body" and "raised
a spiritual body" (p. 98),[6] making the orthodox point that Vanamee will meet Angéle in heaven. Vanamee, however, does not rest
content with such promises. He continues his attempts to call
Angéle from the grave, succeeding ultimately only in the rather hollow victory of calling her daughter from her bed. Father Sarria's
"immovable fact" that the Vision was Angéle's daughter and not
Angéle herself makes absolutely no impression on Vanamee, rapt in
mystical ecstasy, for "Angéle or Angéle's daughter, it was all one."
Vanamee concludes, quoting St. Paul, "Oh, Death, where is thy
sting? Oh, Grave, where is thy victory?" (pp. 268-269). The
rhetorical beauty of this passage should again not blind us to
Vanamee's total misapprehension of what has happened. He has
misinterpreted the parable completely, ignoring Paul's—and Father
Sarria's—point that the resurrected grain of wheat is not "natural"
but "spiritual"; he has, in his own words, found a "Delusion."

The tragedy of both Presley and Vanamee, in sum, is the tragedy
of two men who "Think Big," who deny the forest because they
refuse to admit the existence of trees. Their kindred delusion is
nicely shown in their lunch together in Gaudalajara, where they sit
"out of tune with their world" over their empty wine glasses,
"groping and baffled amidst the perplexing obscurity of the Delusion
[that is, of Vanamee's attempts to call Angéle back from the
grave]" (p. 150), ignoring the sound of the "immovable fact" that
outside the tavern a switch engine is shunting cars in the railroad
yards at Bonneville.

---

[6]Father Sarria here is quoting directly from I Corinthians xv. 36, 44. The
whole parable (I Corinthians xv. 35-50) is the biblical statement of Vanamee's
position. In context, however, Father Sarria and not Vanamee draws the
correct moral.

Within the framework of the novel Vanamee's solution to the problem of the symbolic conflict between the Wheat and the Octopus is also shown to be irrelevant and delusory. Vanamee comes to believe that Death brings forth Life, that, in his compelling phrase, "Time was naught; change was naught; all things were immortal but evil; all things eternal but grief" (p. 268). Nevertheless Norris takes great pains to show that, even if we accept the bringing back to "Life" of Angéle in the person of her daughter as in fact not a delusion, still this is the only time in the book when such a resolution occurs. In contrast to the death and supposed rebirth of Angéle we have the killing of the sheep by the train as a sort of metaphor of the alternative statement to Death's bringing forth Life, the bitter wisdom that one "can't buck against the Railroad," a metaphor which is specifically applied in the futile deaths of Osterman and Harran Derrick and the insanity of Magnus Derrick, and the living death of life imprisonment for Dyke. In none of these cases does Death bring forth Life; and these are peripheral to the main ironic plot analogies between Vanamee, the farmer Hooven, and Annixter. The death of Hooven at the barricade brings about no rebirth at all. His elder daughter, Minna, must sell her body in order to eat and ends symbolically "raped" by the Railroad as Angéle was by the Other; his wife dies of starvation in San Francisco, leaving his younger daughter orphaned. Here Death has brought forth Death, as indeed we would expect. The symbolic analogy to Annixter is much more pointed. Annixter's death not only leaves Hilma bereaved, but the shock causes her to have a miscarriage, a result directly opposite to the general law of life which Vanamee posits on the basis of the delusory rebirth of the second Angéle. It is true in the novel that Death and Life are inextricably related, but certainly not in any such simple fashion as Vanamee supposes. For at the end of *The Octopus* the grave is everywhere victorious in the San Joaquin.

II

If one reads *The Octopus* carefully, one becomes aware of the irony that the only area in the book in which there is substantial philosophical agreement between the Railroad and the farmers concerns the nature of that very Force which Presley finds as the justification of the ways of the P. and S. W. to the ranchers of the San Joaquin. When Shelgrim tells a dumbfounded Presley *"that railroads build themselves,*" that "you are dealing with forces . . . when you speak of Wheat and the Railroads," that "the Wheat is one force, the Railroad another, and there is the law that governs them supply and demand" (p. 395), he is only voicing the opinions of most of the other characters, not all of whom are by any means sympathetic to the P. and S. W. This whole fuzzily optimistic ideal acts throughout the book as a kind of ironic contrapuntal refrain to the real conflict. The first time we meet S. Behrman in Bonneville, in a discussion with Magnus and Harran Derrick which is not marked by any excess cordiality, the only point everyone agrees on is S. Behrman's pompous statement that "The best way is that the railroad and the farmer understand each other and get along peaceably. We are both dependent on each other" (p. 49). That Magnus Derrick accepts this point of view is not, however, particularly startling when we consider that he himself says almost the same thing to his son Lyman, whose election to the Railroad Commission has been compassed by bribery. "Fairness to the corporation," says Magnus sententiously, "is fairness to the farmer" (p. 204). Indeed this argument, not too surprisingly, is often used in the book as a smoke screen by someone who does not want his real motives too thoroughly inquired into. After Osterman has proposed bribing the Railroad Commission, for example, he points out to a doubting Annixter that the farmers and the Railroad need each other. Annixter has objected to Osterman's plan on the grounds that the P. and S. W. would not move the grain at low rates, but, as Osterman says, "Hauling at low rates is better than no hauling at all. The wheat has got to be moved" (p. 74). Even Genslinger, when he comes to blackmail Magnus Derrick, rises to a certain philosophical acumen. "This is an unfortunate business, Governor," he says profoundly, "this misunderstanding between the ranchers and the railroad. . . . *Here* are two industries that *must* be in harmony with one another, or we all go to pot" (p. 309).

The true significance of the argument that the Railroad and the farmers need each other may best be seen by a discussion of the story of Dyke and his ill-fated hop farm. Dyke is the only farmer in the valley who has a good word for the Railroad. He believes, on the basis of a quoted hop rate of two cents a pound, that "the rates on hops *are fair*" (p. 153) and that it is not worth the P. and S. W.'s while to attempt to squeeze such a small operator as he is. When the Railroad increases shipping rates on hops from two to five cents a pound, Dyke is ruined and asks for an explanation of why the P. and S. W. raised the tariff. The clerk says first that the price of hops has gone up to "nearly a dollar." Dyke does not immediately see the logical connection between this fact and the raising of the shipping rates, but the clerk enlightens him. "The freight rate," he says, *"has gone up to meet the price. We're not doing business for our health"* [italics mine]. When Dyke, who still does not understand, asks for a further explanation of the basis for determining freight rates, S. Behrman makes it perfectly clear. Emphasizing "each word of his reply with a tap of one forefinger on the counter before him," he says the basis is "All–the–traffic–will–bear' (p. 239). This is precisely the point of the book. The argument between the farmers and the P. and S. W. is not over whether or not the Railroad performs a valid service in moving goods, but simply about whether or not its rates are exorbitant. The Railroad is not only a Force, as Vanamee and Presley would have it, but a force which operates at a profit, and the ranchers think the profit is excessive. This profit motif provides the basis of the entire argument of the tale, and it is remarkable that it has been so little noticed by critics. When we first meet Harran Derrick, we see him in receipt of a letter from his father telling him that the ranchers have lost their first legal battle to force the Railroad to lower its rates. The judge's opinion in the case was that the grain rates which the farmers suggest would be so low that "the railroad could not be operated at a *legitimate profit*" [italics mine]. This, as Harran sees, is the real point at issue. He picks up the phrase ironically: "Can we raise wheat at a *legitimate profit* with a tariff of four dollars a ton. . .?" (pp. 8-9—italics mine). We first meet S. Behrman engaged in a similar argument over the *fairness* of the Railroad's shipping rates with Magnus and Harran Derrick. "Who is to say what's a fair rate?" Harran asks. S. Behrman replies that "the laws of the State . . . fix the rate of interest at seven per cent. That's a good enough standard for us." It is good enough standard for the ranchers too. But the real problem is how one computes the basis of this supposedly "fair" seven per cent. The ranchers claim that it should be computed on the basis of a construction cost to the P. and S. W. of "fifty-four thousand dollars per mile" while S. Behrman holds that every mile cost the Railroad "eighty-seven thousand" dollars to build. "It makes a difference," as Harran logically concludes, "on which of these two figures you are basing your seven per cent" (pp. 48-49). The argument, then, is not over Force at all, or public service, or private property, but rather over what is a fair profit. The Railroad claims that it cannot lower its rates without going bankrupt; the farmers claim that the profits are exorbitant. The real significance of Presley's interview with Shelgrim, the President of the P. and S. W., at the end of the story lies not in what Shelgrim says but in what he leaves out. Shelgrim concludes his argument by an analogy between the Railroad and the farmers. "Can your Mr. Derrick stop the Wheat growing?" he asks rhetorically. Not staying for an answer he continues: "He can burn his crop, or he can give it away, or sell it for a cent a bushel—just as I could go into bankruptcy—but otherwise his Wheat must grow. Can anyone stop the Wheat? Well, then, no more can I stop the Road" (p. 396). In other words, the P. and S. W. has two options; it can go bankrupt or it can move the wheat on its own terms. But isn't there another option which Shelgrim chooses to ignore? Magnus Derrick does not have to sell the wheat for a cent a bushel; he might sell it for five cents a bushel, or even ten; he might, in short, make a profit on the sale, just as the P. and S. W. might conceivably make a profit on the hauling. Shelgrim does not choose to discuss this possibility and Presley never sees it, even when he discovers the impressive "immovable fact" that the "Force" behind the P. and S. W. not only moves wheat to the starving hordes of China, but asparagus by special train to malnourished Railroad vice-presidents.

The argument of *The Octopus*, in short, is not over Force, at all. The real conflict in the book is understood much better by Mrs. Dyke than by Presley when she tells him that "the men who own the railroad are wicked, bad-hearted men who don't care how much the poor people suffer, so long as the road makes its eighteen million a year" (p. 152). Whether or not this statement, abstractly considered, is correct, it at least shows that Mrs. Dyke understands the problem. And the solution which Norris offers is not to be found in the muddled pseudo-Darwinism philosophy of Vanamee and Presley, but rather in the appeal for social justice in the copybook of Dyke's daughter, the "little Tad," where in strange juxtaposition we find " 'Truth Crushed to Earth Will Rise Again,' 'As for Me, Give Me Liberty or Give Me Death,' . . . 'My motto—Public Control of Public Franchises,' " and " 'The P. and S. W. Is an Enemy of the State' " (p. 151).